Techniques & Designs for Embroidering on Cloth

BEADED
Embellishment

Amy C. Clarke
& Robin Atkins

INTERWEAVE PRESS
www.interweave.com

Editor: Marion Agnew
Photography: Joe Coca, unless otherwise noted
Illustrations: Jay Le Vasseur
Cover design: Susan Wasinger
Book design and production: Dean Howes
Proofreader: Nancy Arndt
Indexer: Judy Berndt

Interweave Press
201 East Fourth Street
Loveland, Colorado 80537-5655 USA
www.interweave.com

Printed in China through Phoenix Offset

Library of Congress Cataloging-in-Publication Data

Clarke, Amy C., 1969-
  Beaded embellishment : techniques and designs for embroidering on cloth a
beadwork? / Amy C. Clarke and Robin Atkins.
       p. cm.
Includes bibliographical references and index.
  ISBN 1-931499-12-8
  1. Beadwork. I. Atkins, Robin, 1942- II. Title.
  TT860 .C553 2002
   746.5—dc21
                              2002007646

10 9 8 7 6 5 4 3 2 1

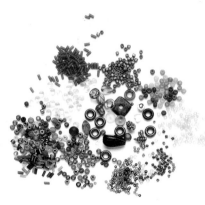

Acknowledgments

I keep thinking about the saying, "On the shoulders of giants, a little person can see a great distance." There are a lot of giants in my life that I'd like to thank: my parents—Mark and Pat Clarke—for teaching me so much, including a love of learning, teaching, literature, art making, and living; my former fibers professors—Mimi Holmes and Tom Lundberg—for pushing me to do my best and for teaching me how to teach through great instruction; Rita Buchanan, for teaching me how to be an editor and a writer; Linda Ligon and Marilyn Murphy, for giving me wonderful opportunities and a great job; Dustin Wedekind, for being an inspiration as well as a friend; Kelly Moore, for encouragement, friendship, and love; Julia Clarke, Evan Clarke-Resendez, Ben Clarke, and Helen Clarke for providing fun and great companionship; and Robin Atkins, for having so much enthusiasm about this book, teaching me so much about beading, and for her beautiful, inspirational style of bead embroidery!

Amy C. Clarke

So many people to thank—so little space! Thanks to my co-author, Amy Clarke—nearly a stranger when she asked me to help her with this book, now a wonderful friend, "birthing partner," and creative inspiration. We do things a bit differently, yet with great respect and admiration for each other. Thanks to everyone who helped us with this book—Val Thorsen for her insightful first-draft editing, the generous artists who allowed us to include photographs of their beadwork, Andrea Adams for helping us with the *9/11 Bead Quilt* photos, Dustin Wedekind for sharing his Sashiko vest project, Valerie Hector and Anna Fehèr for sharing photographs from their private collections, Joyce Herold for showing us the Native American collection at the Denver Museum of Nature and Science, and the staff at Interweave Press for their professional help. Thanks to the beautiful people of Vista for sharing their love and knowledge of beading with me. Thanks to all my bead friends and students for all the countless things I have learned from you. Thanks to my beloved husband, Robert Demar, for his support and encouragement while I sat at the computer for weeks at a time. And finally, thanks to the universe for beads, fabrics, needles, and thread!

Robin Atkins

CONTENTS

INTRODUCTION

ROBIN ATKINS AND I have joyfully filled this book with practical information that you can use to learn how to create with bead embroidery.

However, I must confess that there is nothing practical about the reasons why I started working in fibers and, eventually, beading.

My mother, aunt, and grandmother got me started sewing at an early age. I remember how my grandmother very patiently taught me how to embroider tea towels. At the same time I was reading books about girls my age who spent a portion of every day stitching. I loved the connection I felt to generations of people—within my own family, in the novels, and in history—through the stitches I was making. I was also enamored with fairytales—where common, everyday objects could be imbued with powerful magic that would help the hero overcome incredible odds.

Later, when I was in college studying fibers and art history, I kept coming across passages in books about the spiritual significance of thread and beads. I was fascinated by anthropological studies that told about parents tying a red thread around an infant's wrist to bind the child's soul to the body. Sometimes they tied a bead on the thread to ward off the evil eye. I read about bits of mirror embroidered on textiles from India, also meant to deflect and confuse the evil eye. I pored over texts and photos depicting baby carriers from Indonesia. These baskets were laboriously embellished with beads meant to protect the baby inside from unseen forces.

Slowly, I gathered these stories and began to form my ideas about the compelling need that I (and I was discovering, that a lot of people) have to cover garments and basic household objects with precious stones and pretty glass beads. I asked myself, how could it be that people believed that intricately stitching an object could provide protection from the things they feared? Then I thought about how when I make something, especially when I invest a lot of time and thought in the project, the feelings and ideas that I experienced while making the piece sometimes get caught up in the beads. When I look at the piece again, even years after completing it, I am reminded of those thoughts and feelings; somehow a part of me gets stitched down, too.

Many times, people have looked at my work and claimed that they wouldn't have the patience to do such intricate work. I smile to myself when they say that—I know it has nothing to do with patience. I bead because I'm compelled to bead. It is the balm of my day, it is my connection to generations of stitchers who have come before me, it is the way I make order in my world, and it is how I work through thoughts and feelings.

These are my reasons for beading—but I really don't think anyone needs reasons beyond simply loving to work with beads, threads, and cloth. My hope is that in these pages you'll find the tools and inspiration you need to pursue your own magical journey with beads.

Amy C. Clarke

SEVERAL YEARS AGO, I was asked to talk about Embellishment, an annual bead and button conference, on a morning TV program. As the camera zoomed to a framed piece of my bead embroidery—about 6 inches by 7 inches, and mostly done with size 15° seed beads—the hostess asked me, "So, how many beads are there in this piece, and how many hours did it take to make?"

Somehow, her question sounded like a foreign language—one I didn't know. At the time, I sputtered some answer, saying I didn't count how many beads, probably thousands, guessing the time at around 300 hours. I wanted to explain the joy and fascination of timelessness I sense whenever I let my fingers play with beads. Like a child absorbed with a new toy, I never feel time when I'm stitching beads on cloth. And something else happens too. Numbers, worry, irritations, criticisms, and pettiness fade away; serenity, calm, satisfaction, and delight take over my total awareness.

There in the brightly lit studio, feeling nervous and inadequate for not having precise answers, I couldn't think of a way to turn her questions into an opportunity to explain why I love sewing tiny beads on fabric so very much. For me, the greatest gift of bead embroidery is inner peace. As I stitch bead after bead, I feel that I am ancient, sitting cross-legged under a Cyprus tree—contemplative, whole, complete, and totally honest.

Maybe when you picked up this book, you didn't have any such expectations. Perhaps you like the beautiful work you see here, or you enjoy other types of beading, or you want to sew bead embellishments on quilts or garments. Surely you've already discovered the magic of beads. But as you progress through this book and begin to find your own beaded pathway, there's more in store for you than you may have imagined.

We will teach you how to get started—about fabrics, beads, notions, and supplies; how to organize your workspace; and how to begin sewing beads on cloth. You'll learn the four basic stitches of bead embroidery, many variations, edging and fringing techniques, and methods for finishing your work. You'll have a variety of projects to follow exactly or to serve as a starting point for your own creations. And you'll be inspired by the work of many talented bead embroidery artists in the Gallery section.

But entirely on your own, as you sit and work, sewing bead after bead, you will discover yourself and feel yourself well-placed in the universe. Each of my students over the past decade, in his or her way, has described this phenomenon. It is a gift, yours for the taking. It requires only one thing of you—that you pick up your needle and begin.

Robin Atkins

THE HISTORY OF BEADING ON CLOTH

TRAVEL TO ANY COUNTRY in the world, and you are likely to find men and women beading on cloth, doing what we call "bead embroidery." These individuals can be grouped into three general categories.

- Those in the first and most prolific group live in small rural villages and embellish everyday objects with beads as part of long-standing folk traditions, which can go back several centuries.
- Those in the second group work in small (or occasionally large) factories or loosely assembled groups of home workers, making bead-embroidered items for sale. This group includes designers and artists who create one-of-a-kind pieces, either on commission for wealthy customers or to sell in galleries and exclusive shops.
- Those in the third group tend to live in cities and larger towns, are generally affluent, and work with beads as a hobby. Like most of us, people in this group make beaded objects for personal use and enjoyment.

The more I know about these three groups, the more fascinating it is to speculate about the cross-influences among them. For example, maybe a queen somewhere has a resident artist who adorns her robes with floral embroidery done in tiny pearls. The women of her court appreciate the beauty and style of the artist's work, copy certain aspects of it (perhaps using faux pearls), and adapt the look to their own apparel. Then women of means, traveling to the palace from distant towns, see, copy, and adapt the style for their own clothing, using whatever materials they can afford and find. Finally, peasants and servants of these women, taking note of the new adornment, find some way to incorporate it into their fanciest dresses. By now, the look has changed significantly, and the pearls may be replaced with glass seed beads. But when you look closely, you can see the influence of the original robes worn by the queen. Variations of this hypothetical example have occurred in most countries of the world.

Sometimes influences travel the other way as well, even spreading from one continent to another by means of trade routes. An item made by indigenous village people as part of their ancient folk customs may be adapted and made for export, then copied by hobbyists, who in turn create patterns and directions for it, until it becomes the latest hobby craze. In addition, some fashion designers draw heavily on folk art influences for their creations.

EXAMPLES OF CROSS-INFLUENCE

The beading traditions of Native Americans, especially the Athapaskan tribes, reflect much European influence. These traditions of embellishing cloth with bead-like objects—shells, quills, bird beaks, etc.—go back to antiquity, according to oral and pictorial tribal histories. When early European settlers brought glass beads to trade, many tribes began to substitute the colorful new beads for some of their traditional embellishments.

This influence extended beyond materials. Some tribes began to copy and adapt some of the European patterns and designs. Early missionaries tried teaching Native American women how to do thread embroidery in the styles popular among the educated, upper-class societies of Europe. The Native Americans took those patterns (particularly floral designs) that interested them and adapted them to their own style of embellishment, working them in seed beads rather than thread.

In the early 1900s, Native American tribes of the Northeast woodland areas (especially the Iroquois) adapted the European designs again, forming cottage industries to produce pin cushions, elegant little pillows, and wall hangings to sell to wealthy whites who visited tourist attractions like Niagara Falls. Later these became very expensive, highly collectible treasures, now known as "beaded whimsies."

BEAD EMBROIDERY AS A FOLK ART TRADITION

As noted above, people who do bead embroidery can be grouped into three categories. Of these, the native or village beading traditions are the most stable and long-standing.

Twice I made extended visits to one little village, Vista, located in northwestern Romania, to study with an elderly woman who is considered to be the best beader in town. Vista is populated by about 1,500 Hungarians, the largest ethnic minority of the country.

▼ *A mid-nineteenth century Iroquois bag from New York. Photo courtesy of the Photo Archives department, Denver Museum of Nature and Science, Denver, Colorado, all rights reserved.*

▲ *Beaded Whimsies made by Native Americans in the Northeast United States for the tourist trade near Niagara Falls, New York, from the early 1900s. From the Collection of Janet Stauffacher, Vintage Vogue, Corona, California.*

▼ *A young Hungarian girl in Vista, Romania, wearing the traditional beaded costume of one who is confirmed but not yet married.*

Photo by Robin Atkins

The oldest written documents I could find about the embroidery traditions in Vista date to 1907. Folk artists of the area have recorded details of beaded and embroidered costumes in their paintings, dating back perhaps another 100 years. But according to oral history, the custom of embellishing everyday and dressy clothing with beads, ribbons, and thread embroidery dates back even further. Each year, like rings in the cross-section of an ancient tree, folk customs develop and sometimes shift slightly, reflecting changes in events in their immediate world and in the availability of materials.

The old woman in Vista, who taught me her methods and symbolic images for bead embroidery, told me that 300 years ago, before they had glass beads, women of the village lavishly embellished their aprons, vests, jackets, skirts, blouses, and headdresses with ribbons and thread embroidery. But for reasons she couldn't explain, when the women of the village first discovered beads, possibly 200 years ago, they went "bead crazy." Slowly over the next few decades, they began substituting bead embroidery for thread embroidery.

They even substituted bead embroidery on cloth for items originally made from lace or ribbons. For example, 200 years ago women wore a lace band over their forehead under their wool scarves, possibly to protect their treasured scarves from being soiled by oil from their skin and hair. Sometime in the past 100 or so years, some girl or woman made a panel of bead-embroidered fabric and substituted it for the lace. Quickly, the idea caught the fancy of other women in the village, and now all the headbands are beaded in

a similar manner to the one shown here. The name for this article of clothing translates as "bead lace," a remnant of the past tradition of using lace.

The beaded beads of the tassel pictured here (worn attached to the collar or neck band of women's and girls' blouses) are another example of the transition to beads in Vista. Before the 1940s, the tassels were made with wool yarn pom-poms. The one pictured here is the new style, made by covering wooden beads with yarn needle lace, then stitching beads onto the yarn. It was made by the gnarled hands of a village elder, my teacher, who had once made and worn the pom-pom style as a young girl. She now happily makes the new beaded style.

The apron shown here is from about 1950 and represents another step in the gradual shift from thread embroidery to bead embroidery in Vista. The vertical panels still retain some yarn embroidery, used to provide background color for the beadwork. The horizontal panel in this apron is actually much older than the rest of the apron, probably taken from an older apron made around 1900. Its foundation is a panel of woven netting. The design is made by sewing beads of different colors into the holes of the netting. Notice that some of the holes are filled with thread rather than beads (blue, green, and red), possibly because these colors of beads were not available to the maker. In keeping with the gradual trend toward more and more bead embellishment, the women of Vista today make their apron panels much wider and of solid bead embroidery.

▲ *Beaded tassels from Vista, Romania.*

▲ *A beaded apron from Vista, Romania.*

▲ *A headband embroidered with beads from Vista, Romania.*

▼ *A beaded headdress and throne made in the mid-1900s in Africa for a Yoruba chieftain. From a collection at Karen Murphy's Oasis Bead Lounge, Freeland, Washington.*

Photos by Robin Atkins

These three examples from Vista show how bead embroidery can be a way of life among the rural people in many villages around the world. In Vista, every woman and girl knows how to bead. Every woman and girl can make an apron, a headband, or a beaded tassel—sometimes even more intricately embellished than

▼ *Fragments with counted-thread bead embroidery and bead smocking found in Mexico City, Mexico.*

the ones pictured here. They don't make things to sell; they don't think of beading as a hobby; and it's definitely not a passing fad. In Vista, beading is and has been a way of life for centuries, with the methods and images passed down from one generation to the next. As in Vista, there are living, yet old, beading traditions in many other countries of the world. Village women (and men) in parts of Africa, Eastern Europe, Asia, China, the Middle East, the Arctic, and North and South America still sew beads on everyday objects and clothing as a life-long cultural practice. Here are a few examples from different parts of the world.

In Africa, many tribes have preserved their custom of beading everyday objects (such as baby carriers), apparel and personal adornment (such as the broad collars of the Masai people), and even

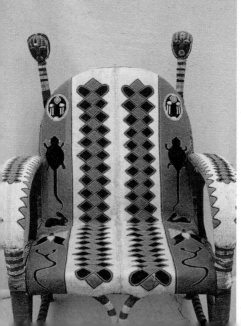

crowns and thrones for tribal leaders. The beaded chair and headdress pictured here were made in the mid-1900s for a Yoruba chieftain.

In some Mexican villages, women embellish their blouses with counted thread bead embroidery (like cross-stitch) and beaded smocking. Because the blouse fragments shown here were purchased along with many others from a street peddler in Mexico City, their exact history and origin are unknown. Looking at all of the fragments (designs, fabrics and beads), it was clear to me that they represent a tradition continuing from the mid-1800s to the present.

In Malaysia and Sumatra, traditional wedding panels feature allegorical designs that may signify the bounty of nature or carry a wish for the couple's fertility. Pictured here is a detail from one such panel from the early twentieth century. The bright colors and sparkling metal sequins brought beauty to the wedding festivities, while the images provided a visual symbolic summary of the event.

The Importance of Beading among Indigenous Folk Artists

Before we leave the subject of indigenous bead embroidery, here are two stories to illustrate how important their beading traditions are to village women.

When I was in Vista, I noticed that it had no stores or commercial structures of any kind and that the people subsisted on a primitive bartering system. Knowing that they rarely traveled beyond

Photo by Eileen Ryan

▲ *A Malaysian or Sumatran wedding panel (detail) from the early twentieth century.*

neighboring villages, I asked where they got their beads. My teacher answered that relatives visiting from bigger cities were often asked to buy and bring beads. In some years, no beads were available, even in the largest cities of Romania. In those years, despite severe governmental restrictions on travel, the village selected a trio of young girls to walk (and occasionally hitch rides with friendly farmers) several hundred miles, all the way to the Czech Republic, to buy beads. Girls were chosen because if they were caught illegally crossing Romania's borders, they would receive less severe punishments than boys or men and could perhaps bluff the officials if they were very clever. Beads were so important to the culture of Vista that the people were willing to take great risks to get them.

While attending a large folk arts festival in Budapest, Hungary, in the mid-1990s, I noticed a small group of costumed women sitting in a little park beading and knitting. They were Natives from Siberia. Several of the women were working on small, fur-trimmed, bead-embellished pieces of wool, which seemed at first to be wall-hangings. After lengthy sign language communication with one of the women, I learned they were making traditional needle and thread keepers, and that she would be willing to sell me one. However, the woman seemed terribly upset about something. She kept putting her tiny bent beading needle in the needle keeper and taking it out while trying to

▼ *A needle keeper made by a native Siberian woman.*

Photo by Robin Atkins

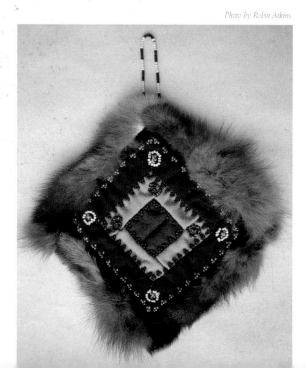

Photo by Robin Atkins

▲ *A native Siberian woman wearing her traditional costume and beads.*

explain something important in her native tongue. With the help of a passer-by who spoke both a little Russian and a little English, I learned that traditionally these keepers were made as gifts and given with a thread tied to a little bone sewn on the back and a needle as symbols of prosperity—always having the needed tools at hand. This woman had only the one needle. In fact, the whole group had only three needles to be shared among them. Thus she could not give (or sell) the piece to me, because it would not be right to do so without a needle attached.

Although my interpreter convinced the woman to sell me the piece without a needle, I returned to the spot the next day of the festival with three packages of St. John's beading needles (75 in all!) and gave them to the woman. At first she didn't know what the package was. I opened it and handed her one needle. After biting it and examining the size of the eye, she began a highly animated conversation with the other women, and eventually divided the needles among them, reserving one entire package for herself. You would have thought I had given her a huge pot of gold!

Beads and beading materials are extremely precious to indigenous beaders, worth taking great risks to get. And even the simplest thing, like a package of needles, is a significant gift to them.

BEAD EMBROIDERY AS A BUSINESS

The second group of beaders, women who work in small factories or home-based businesses making beaded objects to sell, is rather different from groups working in the folk tradition, as described above.

I spent one afternoon in a small, woman-owned business in the Czech Republic that produces beaded evening bags and other beaded evening wear, such as neckties, lapels for jackets, and hats. All the workers sat on hard chairs holding wooden frames vertically in their laps. A heavily starched fabric was stretched over the frames, and the shape to be beaded was drawn on the fabric. Other workers had previously strung combinations of seed and bugle beads, according to a pre-designed pattern, on heavy thread. Using the two-needle couching technique, the workers sewed the strung beads onto the fabric. When the beading was complete, another worker assembled the piece.

Workers beaded the exact same design over and over, for many weeks or months, until work began on some new product. Although I would dislike the repetition of their work, these women were pleased to show me their techniques and were proud of how fast they could complete a large area of beading. They seemed content to sit and talk while working. However, when I asked, they told me they like beads but would not consider beading at home for pleasure.

Photo by Robin Atkins

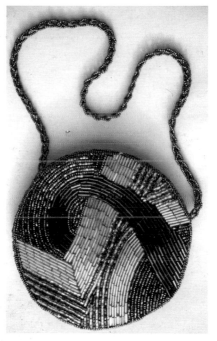

▲ *A beaded evening bag made in a small factory in the Czech Republic.*

▼ *A man's tobacco pouch from mainland China.*

Photo by Valerie Hector

Many inexpensive bead-embroidered goods have been made in this way during the past two centuries. In shops all over the world, we see items like these made in Indonesia, India, China, the Czech Republic, South America, Africa—wherever cheap labor and beads are available. Sometimes the designs are very modern and chic; sometimes they are more ethnic. Generally, the pieces are shockingly affordable to any of us who bead for pleasure and know how much time it takes to make such items and what they would have to cost to yield a fair hourly wage by our standards.

A whole other category of artists and designers do bead embroidery as a business under different circumstances. Designers and artisans in the ateliers of Paris, for example, bead for the haute couture. The firm Lesage is one famous example. Its highly skilled artists make one-of-a-kind pieces for the very famous and affluent for considerably more money than wages common in developing nations.

Artisans who bead for the wealthy are not only modern or Western. Museum collections include many beautiful beaded items from other cultures made by talented artists for prosperous individuals or families. For example, the man's tobacco pouch, pictured here, is from mainland China, probably the Shanghai area. It was made in a very painstaking method—sewing beads one at a time (similar to Peking knots) to create a dense, solid surface—and includes costly foreign materials.

In our country and time, many artists fall somewhere between haute couture designers and factory workers. These artists make one-of-a-kind or limited-production pieces to sell in galleries and art shows. Some barely make a subsistence living; others do quite well.

BEAD EMBROIDERY AS A HOBBY

In most urban cultures during the eighteenth through mid-twentieth centuries, bead embroidery went in and out of fashion with upper-class women, who were required to master the arts. Society women were schooled in some form of sewing or handwork, writing, literature, and music, the specifics of which changed frequently in response to the latest trend. For a few years women might make beaded handbags by knitting or crocheting fine cord, with beads pre-strung on the cord in the desired pattern. Then for the next few years, the trend might be to make cigarette or name-card cases by sewing beads onto evenly punched card stock in a counted-square technique similar to needlepoint. Then, perhaps, for a few decades, thread embroidery would prevail.

These women were the forerunners of the modern-day hobbyist. According to a veteran bead shop owner (half a century in one shop!), beading as a hobby comes and goes in cycles, peaking every fourteenth year. Beading was prevalent in the 1960s for a few years, and a few bead craft books were published at that time. But in 1988, when I started beading full-time, not one beading book was in print. Fourteen years later, in 2002, more than 600 titles are available, and more books are published all the time. Internet bead groups, bead societies, and home gatherings where women do beadwork together (similar to quilting bees) are ubiquitous. Beading appears to be more popular at the turn of the twenty-first century than ever before.

Some bead hobbyists try a little of this and a little of that, often taking classes to learn new beading techniques or patterns. Others settle into one favored method and stick with it for many years. Those who practice bead embroidery and other bead-working methods for a long time, mastering techniques and discovering new ways to express their artistic concepts, are turning what has been considered craft or hobby into a respectable art form.

My personal theory is that the artists emerging from the hobbyists and the indigenous traditions (among them many well-known Native American beaders) are causing beading to become a recognized art form. The recognition of beading as an art form creates the opportunity for exhibitions and competitions, which in turn further elevates both the art and the craft. I believe that the birth of beading as an art is the reason behind the tremendous and sustained interest in beading as a hobby at the turn of the twenty-first century.

Whether you pursue it as a hobby or an art form, bead embroidery can lead to many enjoyable hours and the creation of an exciting assortment of embellished objects and clothing, as you will see in the following chapters of this book! ✦

▼ *A European name-card case, circa 1930.*

Photo by Robin Atkins

GETTING STARTED

ANYTHING GOES!

Of all the different types of beading, stitching beads on fabric is the most flexible. It allows you to use the widest variety of beads, threads, and other materials. This is one of the great appeals of bead embroidery—anything goes!

In bead stringing, every object must have a hole. But in bead embroidery, you can incorporate stone or glass cabochons, feathers, old jewelry pieces, Cracker Jack charms—you name it! You can sew anything to fabric using beads to hold it in place. Unlike most weaving or netting, bead embroidery doesn't require you to worry about consistent bead size, shape, or hole size.

So here is your opportunity to look at your stash (or go shopping!) with no strings attached. It puts a whole new perspective on all those little things you have collected since childhood, without knowing what you might do with them. Suddenly, precious little objects like Grandma's buttons, a set of old ink pen points found at a garage sale, or a miniature guitar from a childhood doll have new meaning and potential. Beads you've saved because you love them, but you haven't been able to use, also show new promise.

Seed Beads

Glass seed beads, so named because they look like seeds—small, rounded, and ranging in size from that of a poppy seed to a sunflower seed—are the main staple of most bead embroidery designs. Their designated size is determined by the outside diameter of the bead, not the hole size. The smallest size manufactured today is size 16°. The most readily available, medium-sized seed bead is size 11°. Larger seed beads, size 8° and 6°, are also common and useful in bead embroidery. Vintage seed beads, from before World War II, come in much smaller sizes, 18°–24°—so small that they challenge even the best eyesight.

Smaller seed beads, sizes 11°–15°, make it possible to get fine detail in a design, while larger beads, sizes 5°–10°, make it possible to cover a lot of fabric relatively quickly. Some artists work almost entirely with the smallest seed beads. Some

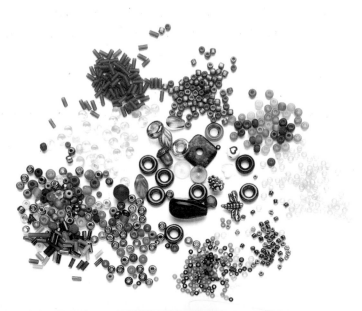

prefer to work with much larger beads. Others use a mix of all sizes and types. Personally, I find a mixture useful and attractive.

As you begin to acquire a palette of seed beads, it will be obvious that both sizes and colors are inconsistent. Take size 11° rounded seed beads, for example—those made in Japan will have larger holes and be slightly more consistent in size than those made in the Czech Republic. Colors vary, too, even from batch to batch by the same manufacturer.

How many different seed beads are available? It's a challenge to estimate—but it's safe to say there are thousands! The astonishing variety of colors and finishes gives an artist an extremely large working palette. All of them may be used in bead embroidery, although colorfastness is a consideration, especially if your creation will be washed or exposed to direct sunlight.

In addition to the typical rounded shape, seed beads may also be triangular, square, tubular, or faceted. *Delicas* are one type of specialty seed beads. Made in Japan and available in a large selection of colors and finishes, these tubular seed beads are very consistent in size and have a comparatively large hole. I tend to use them more often in weaving projects than bead embroidery, but they work well for making a basket weave effect (see page 29) because they are as wide as they are long.

Bugle Beads

Tubular bugle beads, cousins to seed beads, are made in the same way, except that longer pieces are cut from glass tubes and the edges are not usually rounded. The diameter of bugle beads is often about the same as a size 11° seed bead; the length can range from ⅛ inch to 2 inches; the surface may be plain or twisted.

Using bugle beads in bead embroidery creates visual interest, because they have more mass than seed beads. However, because they tend to have sharp edges, which can cut the sewing thread, and can break easily (such as when the cloth is folded), it's important to take a few precautions.

- Look for bugle beads with less-sharp edges. Some manufacturers treat the tubes after cutting them to collapse (or round) the edges slightly.
- When sewing bugle beads on cloth, bracket them with seed beads, so that the thread doesn't touch the edge of the tube (see page 27).

Tests for Color Permanence of Seed Beads

Test your beads before you begin the project. If none of these tests affects the bead color and finish, then the finished item will probably last and wear well over time.

- First, put a few beads on a needle or pin and file the surface with a nail file. Most painted finishes will flake off immediately with this test.
- Next, soak a few beads in water for a day or two. At the same time, put a few beads in a tray in direct sunlight.
- Finally, try soaking a few beads in acetone or nail polish remover.
- If beads are to be sewn on a garment that will be dry cleaned, sew samples of each bead type on a sample of the fabric and have it dry cleaned.

Novelty or Accent Beads, Charms, and Doodads

You may use just about everything and anything in bead embroidery. Glass flowers and leaf-shaped beads (see page 73) are great favorites of mine. Other things I use frequently are small glass rings (which I add to surface loop-fringe), buttons, glass or shell cabochons, bone or shell discs, pearls, metal charms, feathers, and a variety of pressed glass shapes.

If you don't have a collection of small accent beads, you might consider a visit to a bead shop to pick up a few things you like. Antique stores, thrift shops, and yard sales are also great sources for "stuff"—everything from old game pieces (Clue, Monopoly, Scrabble) to jars of old buttons may find a place in your work.

- Use common sense about visual scale. For example, if you are making a small amulet bag (see page 55), you might decide against large beads or metal charms. But if you are making a large bag (see page 66), you can feel free to choose a big button or heavy bead to accent your work.

- Use common sense about weight and dimensions. For example, if you are making a bead-embellished vest (see page 78), you probably won't want to sew a large, lumpy bead or charm on the back, where it will hurt if you lean against it.

- Most metals will eventually tarnish and corrode. When sewn to cloth, the corrosion may discolor or even rot the fabric over time. Take this characteristic of metal objects into consideration when using metal beads and charms in bead embroidery.

CLOTH

You can use beads to embellish any fabric, from the most delicate organza to thick-surfaced cloth like velveteen, heavy upholstery fabrics, or denim or knitted fibers in a sweater. However, if you are just beginning, the easiest cloth to work on is quilting-weight cotton. In the Techniques chapter, we suggest making a sampler using all the techniques for practice and reference. A medium-weight cotton fabric is a good choice for your sampler.

Woven Fabrics

Woven fabrics (such as cotton, linen, polyester blends, wool, rayon, and silk) may be light, medium, or heavy in weight; plain or patterned; textured or smooth; washable or dry clean only. All of them are suitable for bead embroidery, but consider your personal preferences and the eventual use of your project.

- I find printed cottons very inspiring. The designs, color, and "personality" of the print influence the scale, colors, flow, and mood of my work and frequently help me explore unexpected artistic paths.

- For an exciting possibility, try layering fabrics, such as a light organza over a silk brocade. Or bond light-weight silks together using fusing materials available at fabric stores.

- Specialty fabrics, such as Aida or Hardanger cloth, available from needlework shops, have an even thread count (the same number of threads per inch across both the length and width of the fabric), which makes it useful for counted-thread patterns using cross stitch (see pages 28 and 52).

Non-Woven Cloth

Felt, piano felt, and Ultrasuede® are three non-woven materials that are useful for bead embroidery. Although not technically cloth, leather, buckskin, and smoke-tanned hide are also examples of non-woven surfaces that are frequently used for bead embroidery. Because these materials tend to be more stable than woven fabrics, it's not usually necessary to use a hoop or backing to keep your work from puckering.

Other Surfaces for Bead Embroidery

Several times during recent history, it has been popular to embellish knitted sweaters with beads. Knitted fabrics, such as T-shirts, can also be decorated with bead embroidery. The important thing to remember with knitted fabrics is that they stretch easily, making control difficult and puckering likely. However, it just takes a little practice.

It may help to use a stabilizer (such as paper, interfacing, or a non-stretch woven fabric) under stretch fabrics, although under clothing, this layer can make the garment look too stiff.

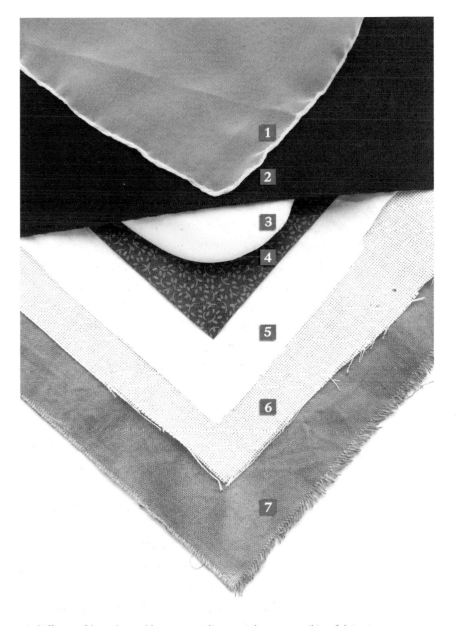

1. chiffon, 2. felt, 3. knitted lycra, 4. medium-weight cotton quilting fabric, 5. cotton muslin, 6. Hardanger cloth, 7. cotton canvas.

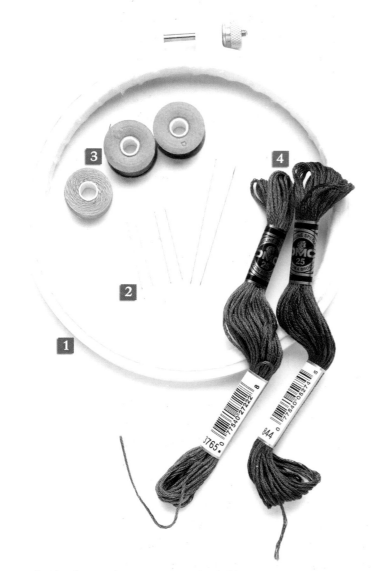

1. embroidery hoop with inner ring covered with fabric, 2. size 12 and size 11 sharps, size 10 beading needles, 3. size D Nymo thread, 4. embroidery floss.

Paper is also easily embellished with bead embroidery. For example, collage artists may add beads (using single stitch and other simple stitches) to layered papers or photographs. Sometimes it is necessary to pre-punch the paper in the desired pattern or at least use a thimble to help push the needle through layers of paper.

NEEDLES

Beading needles, available from bead shops and some craft supply and fabric stores, have the same numbering system as beads. Thus, supposedly you'd need a size 15 needle to work with size 15° seed beads. This relationship isn't always accurate, because the bead size is determined by the outside diameter, not the hole size. However, it's a good place to start.

If you plan to use a lot of size 11° seed beads for your project, begin with a size 11 beading needle. Sometimes the holes are too small, in which case try a size 12 needle, the next size smaller. When you're working with larger beads that have large holes, ordinary hand-sewing, quilting, or embroidery needles also work.

In addition to the designated size, beading needles are available either long (about 2½ inches) or short (about 1 inch). Long needles are more flexible and tend to bend more easily than short ones, especially when you're working on stiff fabrics. Therefore, I prefer the short needles (often called sharps). But either type will do the job.

THREADS

The thread should be strong enough to hold the beads in place over time. Once again, common sense is important. If you are making a small, framed piece using only small seed beads, the thread strength isn't too important. But if you are making a garment, such as a jacket, that will be worn, washed, and handled, thread strength is an important consideration.

The appearance and color of the thread are generally not very important because the thread is hardly noticeable in most bead embroidery stitches. However, if you're beading with transparent beads, the thread color will show through the beads and may change the apparent color or value of your beads. Sometimes you might use a particular color of thread with transparent beads to achieve a color that isn't otherwise available.

The type of thread—natural or synthetic—is another consideration. For projects where the thread shows, such as the coin purse (see page 52), consider using natural cotton or silk embroidery floss, which is available in a great range of beautiful colors. But for most bead embroidery (where the thread doesn't show), we recommend one of the synthetic beading threads, which are stronger than natural threads, impervious to rot, and don't tangle like standard machine-sewing threads.

If your choice of synthetic threads comes in various sizes, choose the largest that will fit through the eye of the needle you intend to use. For example, Nymo, a readily available brand of nylon beading thread, comes in sizes 00 (smallest), 0, A, B, D, and F (largest). Size D, which will fit through the eye of a size 12 or larger beading needle, is a good choice for most bead embroidery projects.

🐚 Measure and cut a working length of thread (about 20 inches) from the spool or bobbin; grasp the thread, one end in each hand; and pull in opposite directions to give it a good stretch. This will straighten the thread and make it less likely to tangle while sewing.

🐚 When threading the needle, if one end of the thread frays easily, try the other. If you still have difficulty, try turning the needle over; because the eye is tapered, the eye is larger on one side than the other. Another useful tip for threading the needle is to moisten the eye of the needle rather than the tip of the thread.

WAXING

Before synthetic threads were invented, cotton, linen, flax, and silk threads were used for needlework, including bead embroidery. All natural-fiber threads are subject to rot over time and in humid climates. Coating these threads with wax slowed the inevitable damage from moisture.

Waxing synthetic threads (such as Nymo), which are not subject to rot, is not necessary. Wax can cause problems in bead-embroidered pieces because it builds up on the surface of the fabric and attracts dirt. Therefore, coating the entire length of a synthetic thread is not recommended. However, coating just the tip of a length of synthetic thread may make threading the needle easier.

STABILIZERS

Unless the fabric is very stiff (such as denim), even experienced bead embroidery artists need something to stabilize the cloth to keep it from puckering. Several methods are available, all of which work for most applications. Once again, the choice is a matter of personal preference.

Paper Backing

For any non-clothing projects, a piece of paper basted to the underside of your fabric magically keeps your tension even and eliminates puckering. Acid-free interleaving paper, available from art supply stores, is the perfect weight and is easily pierced by your needle. Plain typing or computer paper or even notebook paper will also do the job, although the acid in these papers may eventually damage your fabric. Initially the paper will seem a bit stiff, but as you handle it and stitch through it, the paper softens until it is barely noticeable.

Embroidery Hoops

Available in a variety of sizes at fabric shops, embroidery hoops keep your fabric taut while you work. Before using a hoop, wrap a length of ½-inch-wide cotton cloth evenly around the inside ring and stitch it in place. This lining will help keep the fabric in place as you work. Lightly stretch your beading fabric over the inside hoop; then put the larger hoop over the fabric and tighten the fastener.

- If the fabric is stretched too tightly, its fibers will recover when removed from the hoop, causing puckering.
- If possible, choose a hoop that is larger than your finished project. If you have to reposition the hoop after completing part of your piece, open the hoop wide enough to accommodate any beads that may fall between the hoops, and then tighten the hoop. The fabric wrapping on the inside hoop will protect the beads between the hoops as long as you don't force the hoop over the beads.
- When you're beading on ready-made garments of lightweight or translucent fabric, adding paper or fabric stiffeners on the underside would disturb the flow of the garment. In this case, a hoop is a reasonable choice for stability.

Fabric Stiffeners

Buckram, pellon, felt, and various woven or non-woven interfacings, available at fabric shops, can be used as backing for lighter-weight fabrics. Water-soluble stiffeners, which may provide enough stability for some fabrics, are a good choice for sparse designs on garments where permanent backings would cause the garment to look stiff or to flow improperly. Use any of these solutions that will stabilize your fabric so that your work won't pucker. Baste it to the underside of your fabric before you begin to bead.

WORKING SURFACE AND BEAD STORAGE

If you've been beading for a while, you probably already have a way that you prefer to work and a satisfactory system for storing your beads. If you're completely new to beading and want some ideas, here's the way that works best for me.

I work on a beading cloth, hemmed, about 15 inches square, which I made from a natural-color, heavyweight, smooth-surfaced cotton. In tight spaces, such as when beading on airplanes, I use a small cloth handkerchief. I fold the cloth in half and place it on the beading table with the fold toward me, which keeps the beads from rolling off the edge of the cloth. I empty a teaspoon or so of the beads I want to use onto the cloth, maintaining separate piles for each color.

Some beaders prefer working on a tray lined with Ultrasuede®, felt, or cloth. Others like to place their beads in a partitioned glass dish of the type used by watercolor artists. There isn't one best way; it's just a matter of what is convenient for you.

❧ To pick up one bead from a pile on the cloth, touch the hole of a bead with the tip of your needle and scoop it onto the needle with your finger.

- To pick up a few beads of the same color all at once, dome the pile of beads, and pass the needle through the center of the pile. Generally your needle will catch from one to five beads at a time.
- Use a bead scoop or small souvenir spoon to transfer the beads back into your storage containers when you've finished with a color or need to put away your work.

Bead storage is another matter of personal preference and convenience. Many fancy storage systems are available at bead, fabric, and quilting shops—partitioned boxes, screw-together canisters, tiny round tins with glass lids, etc. Some beaders keep their beads in the original tubes or containers so they always know the source (in case they need more). Personally, I've settled on plastic Zip® bags, 1½ inches by 3 inches by 4 millimeters thick. They take up less space than other systems I've tried, are easily portable, and enable me to see the bead colors.

- Although many seed beads are packaged loose in tubes or other containers, some beads come pre-strung in hanks of 10 or 12 strands. Generally I cut the threads at the bottoms of the loops and store the beads in plastic bags. However, some beaders apply pre-strung beads to their work using the string from the hank, and couch them down with a second needle and thread (see page 31). The only caution here is to make sure the threads used by the bead manufacturer to string the hanks are strong enough.

Bead embroidery can be a very portable art. Simply select a few containers of beads you might like to use, prepare your fabric, add your favorite notions, put it all in a small box or bag, and you're ready to bead anywhere. I regularly do bead embroidery on airplanes, during meetings, while visiting my family, and in coffee shops!

LIGHTING AND SEATING

Good lighting and a comfortable chair with back support are important for bead embroidery. It's so easy to sit and work for hours at a time, and before you know it, your eyes feel grainy and your neck is stiff. Periodic stretching, walking, and looking into the distance are gifts to your body and your eyes.

People often comment that I must have really good eyes to do this work. They mean I must have good eyesight, which I do not have. However, I do have excellent glasses, with slightly more magnification at my working distance than normal. If you show and tell your optometrist about your bead embroidery, you can make the most of your eyesight.

CLEANING AND LAUNDERING

Because many washable fabrics shrink slightly when washed for the first time, it's always a good idea to wash fabric before you begin your bead embroidery. If you are making a garment or planning to add beads to a new ready-made garment, it is especially important to wash the fabric or gar-

ment before beading. Use whatever detergent and method of washing and drying you plan to use after the garment is beaded.

To launder garments or objects after they have been embellished with beads, it is safest to use a mild soap or detergent. Place the item in a mesh bag suitable for washing lingerie and machine-wash on the gentle cycle. Spread the item on a flat surface to dry.

- If you haven't pre-tested your beads for color permanence (see page 15), be aware that some colors or finishes may not survive the wash.
- Some fabrics have special washing requirements (dry cleaning, hand washing, or water temperature). Be sure to check the label before machine washing.
- If the garment or item needs ironing after it is washed, use the lowest temperature possible. Place the item bead-side down on several layers of terrycloth toweling and iron on the back only. Be especially cautious if you've used a nylon thread, such as Nymo, because nylon melts at a very low temperature. Test the iron temperature by ironing a loose piece of thread over a scrap of your fabric. If the thread melts, try a lower temperature, or put a layer of cloth between the iron and the thread.

READY, GET SET, GO!

If you've read through all of the above information about beads, fabrics, notions, and preparations for beading, you know far more than most of the artists whose work you see in the Gallery section knew when they first began beading on cloth. Certainly you know more than either of your authors, who both began with the motto "Just DO it!" So now it's your turn to pick up your beads and start stitching them onto your favorite fabric!

TECHNIQUES

Make a Sampler

As you go through this chapter, we recommend trying out all the stitches on a single piece of fabric that you keep on hand as a reference. Cut a piece of plain cotton fabric and a piece of acid-free interleaving paper (if you have it) or notebook paper, each 5 inches square. Baste them together. The paper on the back of your sampler will stabilize your work and keep it from puckering. Later, when you're designing your own pieces, you can look back to your sampler to spark inspiration or remind you how to do a particular stitch.

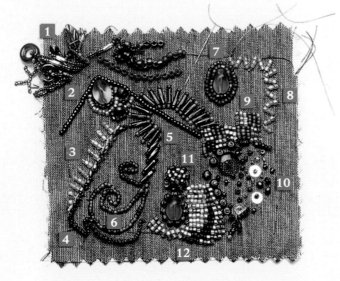

1. fringe, 2. couching around larger beads, 3. buttonhole stitch, 4. picot edging, 5. lazy stitch pathway with bugle beads, 6. back stitch, 7. couching around a larger bead, 8. fly stitch, 9. basket weave with lazy stitch, 10. single stitch, 11. barnacle with stacked single stitch, 12. lazy stitch.

FOUR BASIC STITCHES AND A FEW VARIATIONS

Bead embroidery is both straightforward and easy to learn. There are only four basic stitches: single stitch, lazy stitch, back stitch, and couching! Of course, each stitch has many variations. As you learn and practice them, you may find yourself drawn toward certain stitch variations. By repeating your favorites, you'll give your work its own individual character. Once you've mastered the four basic stitches and a few variations, you'll be able to make almost anything you can imagine with bead embroidery.

PREPARING TO BEAD

Take a needle. Both Robin and I like size 11 sharps—but any needle that you can thread and that will fit through your beads will work. Cut a length of Nymo or your preferred beading thread about 20 inches long. Thread the needle so that you have a long end and a short end. Make a knot in the long end (see page 25 for how to make knots).

SINGLE STITCH

Single stitch (also called seed stitch) seems very simple, yet it can be used to create a wonderful overall texture of bumps or straight and regular repeated patterns. It looks like a French knot in

Knots

Making Knots

Here's a quick and easy way to make a knot that will stay. It is similar to making a French knot in embroidery. As shown in Figure 1, hold the tail of the long end against the needle between your thumb and forefinger. Wrap the thread around the needle 4 times (Figure 2). Hold the wrapped section with your thumb and forefinger and pull the needle through the wrapped section (Figure 3). Keep pulling the needle until the knot is tight at the end of your thread.

Knotting Off

When you have about 4 or 5 inches of thread left, it is time to knot off (Figure 4). On the underside of your fabric, take a small stitch (points *b* and *c* in Figure 4) near the point where your thread exited (*a* in Figure 4), preferably under a bead so the knot doesn't show on the topside. Pull your thread through, but not all the way through—leave a loop and go through the loop 2 times (Figures 5 and 6). Put your thumb and forefinger over the knot and pull your thread tightly against the fabric to secure the knot. Bury the tail by weaving under your stitches about ¾ inch away from your knot, and cut the thread.

- Knot off between stitches if you're going to travel 1 inch or more across the fabric.
- Knot off between stitches if you are making fringe or securing beads that are in danger of being broken off. This way, you lose only that one bead or fringe, which makes repairing the item much easier.

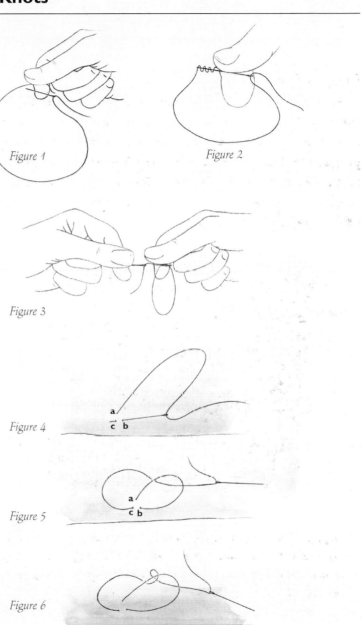

Figure 1

Figure 2

Figure 3

Figure 4

Figure 5

Figure 6

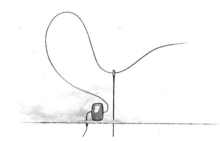

1. single stitch, 2. stacked single stitch, 3. cross stitch.

embroidery. Knot your thread and come up from the back of your fabric (see page 20 for how to prepare your fabric for beading), and pull your needle and thread all the way through to the other side. Tug on the thread to make sure your knot holds. Now pick up one bead with your needle. Push the bead to the fabric and hold the thread tautly in the direction you want your stitch to go. Place the nee-

dle in the fabric close to bead and perpendicular to the cloth. Pull the needle and thread all the way through to the other side. There—you've made a single stitch! That is the first of four basic ways to make bead embroidery stitches. Of course the fun in single stitch is grouping all those single stitches to create patterns, textures, or lines—the possibilities are limitless.

You can do a lot of things with single stitch.

- Scatter your single stitches like seeds across your fabric—randomly coming up, picking up a bead, and stitching it down.

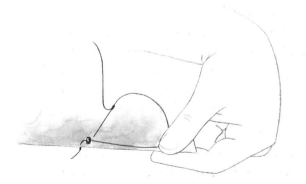

- Make single stitches in a tidy row—follow a line in the pattern of your fabric, a seam on a garment you're embellishing, or create your own line of stitches.
- Vary the size of the stitch, allowing more or less thread to show.

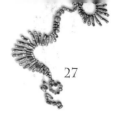

- Vary the spacing between the stitches. Try packing many single stitches into a small space, so that the fabric is almost completely covered. Next, see how far apart you can space the stitches and still create the feeling of having covered an area with a stitch.
- Use single stitch for quilting—add one bead per stitch.

Stacked Single Stitch

Now that you've covered the surface of your fabric with many little stitches, consider moving up. Make a stacked single stitch by coming up through the fabric and picking up 2 or more beads. Skip the last bead you picked up, and go back down through the remaining stack of beads and the fabric. Pull the string taut so that the bead you skipped on

the way back down lies on its side. It will be the anchor for your stack. When you go back down, you can change the position of the stack slightly by placing the needle in the fabric a little distance away from where you came up. Use stacked single stitch to add texture, create fringe, or surround larger

beads. As is true for many of these stitches, you may find that it is hard to stop once you start!

- Try stacked single stitch with 5 or 6 beads to make a tall column of beads. Cluster these stacks—you'll have a wonderful grass-like texture.
- Pick up a size 4°, then size 6°, then size 8°, then size 11°, then size 15° bead to create a stack that sits like a snowman.
- Use a bugle bead to create a stacked single stitch. Remember that bugle beads are sometimes sharp because of the way they are made (see page 15)—so protect your thread by sandwiching your bugle bead between two rounded seed beads.
- Use a thread that is a complementary color (colors that are on opposite sides of the color wheel—see page 85) to the beads—it will show up on the top of the stack and provide visual interest. We talk a little more about complementary colors and the color wheel in the Design chapter.
- Create a raised surface texture that looks like a barnacle (as Robin calls them) by making a

bunch of stacked single stitches in a circle or oval. Then come up through the first stacked single stitch and pass back through the anchor bead at the top of each stacked single stitch. Go back down through the second stack and pull tightly to bring the tops close together. Knot off. Use the barnacle to encase a treasure or as a bezel for a flat-bottom cabochon shape.

Cross Stitch

Some bead embroidery stitches, like cross stitch, use the thread as a decorative element of the stitch. Use colorful Nymo or 2 strands of embroidery floss.

The first step is to stitch the first line of the X. Secure the thread and come up from the underside of the fabric at point *a* (Figure 1). Pick up one bead and go down into the fabric at a diagonal

from where the thread is secured (*b* in Figure 1). Your stitch should be long enough to accommodate three beads. Come up through the fabric directly below the end of your previous stitch and in a straight line from where the needle first came up (*c* in Figure 1). Repeat steps one and two until

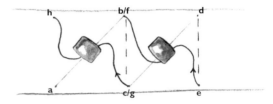

Figure 2

you've completed a row or wish to change the thread color.

The second step is to cross the X. Go back along the row you just made and cross the first lines. Figure 2 shows your thread path. Come up at point *e*, go through the bead, and go back down into the fabric at point *f*. Come up again at point *g*, go through the bead, and go back down into the fabric at point *h*. With each stitch, when you pull the thread through to the back, the bead will be centered in the middle of the two crossed lines of thread (Figure 3).

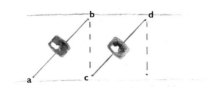

Figure 1

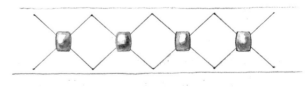

Figure 3

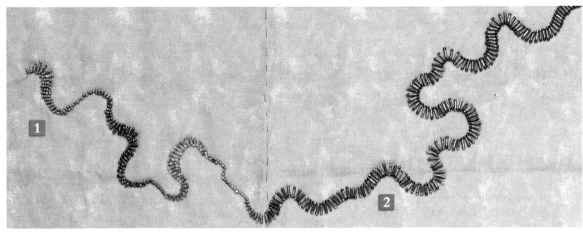

1. lazy stitch pathway, 2. lazy stitch pathway with bugle beads.

LAZY STITCH

Lazy stitch is frequently used to fill an area already defined by some other stitch. It is similar to the satin stitch in thread embroidery. You can also use it to create beaded pathways, as well as thick and thin lines, through your piece. It's great for making borders.

Secure your thread, come up through the underside of the fabric at point *a*, and string 5 beads.

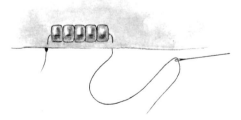

Hold the thread taut with your thumb and gently push the beads back on the thread with your needle, then go down into the fabric right next to the

last bead you strung (point *b*), making sure that the needle goes in perpendicular to the fabric. Come up one bead's width from point *a* (at *c*) and string the next 5 beads.

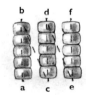

🦋 Lay down groups of lazy stitch at perpendicular angles to create a basket weave effect.

◉ Create a simple pathway by moving the point where you come up through the fabric. When making a curved pathway, come up on

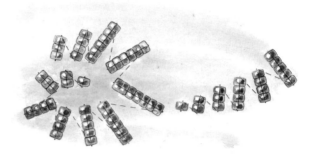

the inside of the curve to keep the pathway even. When the inside of the curve changes to the other side, come up on the other side.

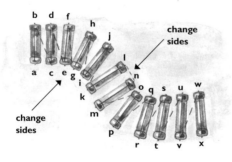

◉ Use bugle beads between 2 seed beads (to protect the thread from the sharp edges on bugle beads) to make a bugle bead pathway.

◉ Change the number of beads gradually in each line of lazy stitch in a pathway to create a meandering line that changes thickness.

◉ Vary the spacing between each line of lazy stitch—experiment with how much fabric you show between each line of lazy stitch.

◉ Create a flower shape by making a tight circle of lazy stitch.

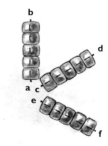

◉ Make a running stitch with lazy stitch. Start at point *a*, string 5 beads, complete the stitch, come up at point *b* and repeat. (See the quilted vest project on page 78.)

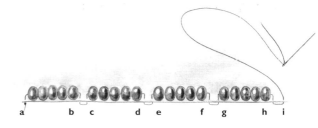

🐚 Make a herringbone stitch using lazy stitch. Start at point *a*, string 5 beads, go in at point *b*, and come back up at point *c*. Criss-crossing over the thread at the beginning of each stitch will help keep the beads in place. You can use the herring-bone stitch as a zigzag line or fill it in to create a pattern.

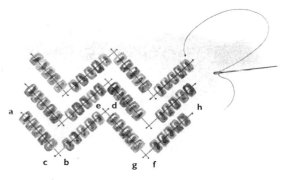

BACK STITCH

The back stitch is great for making straight, continuous lines of beads and curved lines. Use this stitch for outlining shapes or filling large areas.

Secure your thread, come up through the underside of the fabric, and *string 5 beads. Hold the thread taut with your thumb, gently push the

Problem-Solving

Beads Do Not Lie Flat

If your lines of lazy stitch do not lie flat—or if you can see the hole in the last bead you strung because it won't sit up with the rest of the beads—then you need to give the line of beads a little more thread to sit on. When you string your beads and put your needle into the fabric to complete the stitch, make sure that the needle is perpendicular to the fabric when it goes into the fabric.

too close

Beads Are Loose on the Thread

If the beads move around on the thread, the stitch uses too much thread for the number of beads. When you complete a stitch, put the needle into the fabric a little closer to the beads so that the beads are snug on the thread without crowding each other.

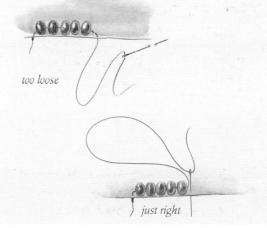

too loose

just right

beads back on the thread with your needle, and go down into the fabric at the end of the line. Come up right behind the second-to-the-last bead, taking care not to pierce the thread. Go through the last two beads and repeat from *. Stitching back through the last two beads helps the beads sit securely on the fabric and makes it possible to curve the line. Once you've made a line of beads with back stitch, you can smooth the curve or straight-

en the line by passing back through the entire line one or more times.

Spacing between Rows of Back Stitch

If you're using back stitch to fill in an area, the spacing between rows of back stitch becomes as important as the spacing between individual beads. Rows that are packed closely may lie flat until several rows are stitched down, and then beads in the first rows may start to pop up—this is especially likely to happen when you start in the center and work out in a spiraling pattern. If you space the beads farther apart, the fabric below may show through. You may want to create a subtle

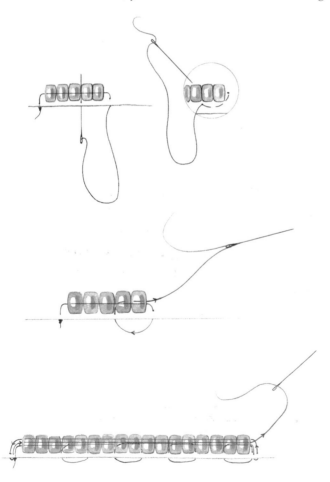

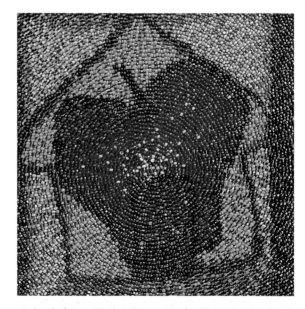

A detail of Amy Clarke's Door, Apple, Core *showing beads that are packed closely (from the collection of Dale Zitek).*

A detail of Amy Clarke's The Juniper Tree *showing beads that are spaced farther apart.*

texture by making the beads pop up or use the foundation fabric as part of the design. However, if you'd like to avoid either situation, make a couple of sample pieces and experiment with row spacing until you are able to get the effects you want.

COUCHING

The name *couching* comes from thread embroidery, where decorative threads are tacked or "couched" onto the background with small stitches that cross the thread. Similarly, in bead embroidery, use little stitches to couch a straight or curved line of beads onto your fabric. You can use the thread as a decorative element in couching by choosing a thread in a contrasting color or value to the beads or fabric.

The two different methods of couching—single-needle and double-needle—both accomplish the same results.

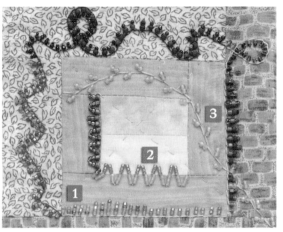

1. buttonhole stitch, 2. fly stitch, 3. feather stitch.

Single-Needle Couching

String enough beads to complete the full length of the line you want to create. Lay down the beads on the fabric and insert the needle into the fabric at the end of the line. Working your way back from the end of the stitch toward the beginning of the line, come up between (and slightly to one side of) the fourth and the fifth beads from the end.

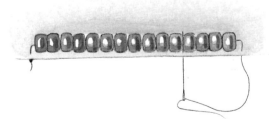

Cross over the stringing thread and go down into the fabric. Proceed along the line of beads, tacking

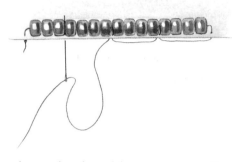

down the thread between every 3 to 5 beads; couch more frequently in curved lines. Be sure that the beads have enough room to sit comfortably on the thread.

To make a curved line, use the thumb of the hand that is not holding the needle to push the beads into the shape you want to create. Hold the beads in place as you couch back around the curve. When you make a curved line, you need to anchor the thread in the fabric a shorter distance from the origination point than when you make a straight line—

you need to allow room for your thread to curve along the path you are beading.

🌑 Use couching to encircle a large bead or cabochon with an even, snug row of beads.

Variations on Single-Needle Couching

Here are some variations of couching that are similar to embroidery stitches. Consider using the thread as a decorative element with these stitches.

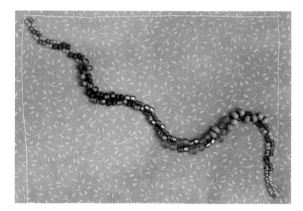

chain stitch.

Chain Stitch

In chain stitch, you make interconnected loops to create a double line of beads. Knot your thread, come up through the fabric at point *a* and string 4 beads. Go down through the fabric at point *b* and

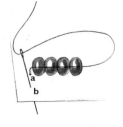

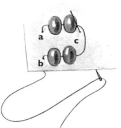

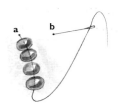

come up at point *c*. String 4 more beads and go down at point *d*. Notice how the stitch is anchored at points *c* and *d*. To end the line of chain stitch, anchor the thread by coming up at point *e* and going down at point *f* without stringing any beads.

beads. Go into the fabric at point *b* and come out at point *c*. Tack down the stitch at point *d*.

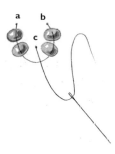

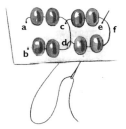

- It is easy to create a checkerboard pattern using chain stitch by alternating colors or values of the beads as you string them.
- Vary the number or size of beads you string to vary the appearance of the chain stitch line.

Fly Stitch

Fly stitch is similar to chain stitch, except that instead of creating a continuous line, the fly stitch creates individual U-shaped stitches. Several fly stitches placed side by side create a decorative border. Come up through the fabric at point *a* and string 4

Feather Stitch

Feather stitch looks like a garland or a branch. Knot your thread and come up at point *a* (see page 36). String 2 beads and go down at point *b*. Come up at point *c*—make sure that the beads are sitting on the thread that goes between points *a* and *c*. String 2 beads and go into the fabric at point *d*.

Come up at point *e* to anchor the stitch, this time making sure that the beads are sitting on the thread that goes between points *d* and *e*. Repeat these steps in a straight or curving line.

- The thread is an important element of this stitch—it works especially well with 2 strands of embroidery floss. Use a size 10 beading needle when you're using embroidery floss.
- To give the feather stitch some depth, try using two similar hues and shades of a thread, rather than two strands of the same color thread. From a distance the thread will look like the same color, but up close, the subtle variations will be visible.
- Do the same with the beads—choose beads from the same color family, but in slightly different shades or different finishes.

Buttonhole Stitch

Buttonhole stitch makes a great edging. Knot your thread and come up through your fabric at point *a*. String two beads, go down at point *b*, and come up at point *c* to catch the thread and start the next stitch. Make sure that the beads are sitting on the part of the thread that goes between points *b* and *c*. String 2 beads and go down at point *d*, coming up at point *e* to anchor the thread and start the next stitch.

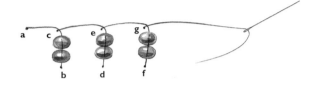

- Vary the number or size of beads (and the length of the stitch between points *b* and *c* to accommodate the beads) to create an undulating line or a line of varying thickness.

- To join two pieces of fabric at an edge using buttonhole stitch, hold the two pieces of fabric together and stitch through both thicknesses as you make each stitch.

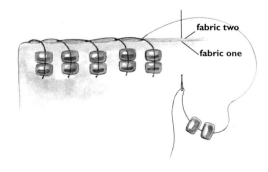

Double-Needle Couching

Double-needle couching (also called two-needle appliqué) uses two needles and threads to couch—one thread to carry the line of beads, and a second thread to couch the beads down. The couching thread can be a decorative element. For example, if you use a thicker thread, such as embroidery floss, the little anchoring lines will show up subtly beneath the beads and change the appearance of the beadwork.

When you use two needles to couch, you secure the thread that the beads are strung on and hold the beads in a line as you tack the thread down with the second thread and needle.

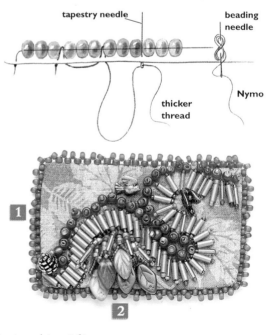

1. picot edging, 2.fringe.

FRINGES AND EDGINGS

Generally, we think of fringes and edgings as decorative elements that we might add to a finished piece of bead embroidery. However, when worked on the surface of bead embroidery, they provide texture and dimension. Use fringes and edgings to frame a piece. The fringe or edging can be applied to a flat piece of cloth or a three-dimensional shape. You can also use a fringe or edging to sew a backing cloth to a piece and to finish an edge or seam, both at the same time (see page 40).

Basic Fringe

Basic fringe is just a longer version of the stacked single stitch (see page 27). It can be a little more floppy than stacked single stitch, or you can pull the tension tight to make the fringe stand at attention.

To make basic fringe, knot your thread and come up through the fabric. String enough beads to make

the length of fringe you desire. Skipping the last bead strung, go back along the stack of beads and through the fabric. Adjust the tension of your fringe by holding onto the last bead (the anchor bead) with one hand while pulling on the thread from the back side. Because most threads stretch slightly over time, we recommend pulling your fringe until it looks just a little too snug. It will soon relax. Knot off, move to the next spot, and knot off again to start the next basic fringe. Knot off before and after making each fringe so that if the piece catches on something and the fringe breaks, you lose only that one fringe. Knotting off after each fringe also helps keep the tension even on all of the fringe.

Adding Charms or Large Beads to Fringe

Add charms or large beads to the basic fringe by creating a loop to hold the charm. Knot your thread and come up through your fabric. String a number of beads until you almost have the length you'd like for your fringe. String 6 beads that are a size or two smaller than the beads in the main part of the fringe. Add the charm and string 6 more small beads. Go back through the entire stack of larger beads to the fabric; then go through the fabric, adjust the tension, and knot off on the back.

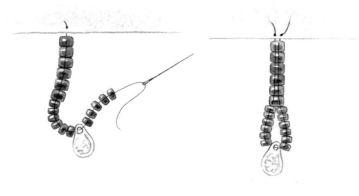

You may need to vary the number of small beads to accommodate the charm or large bead so that it will hang comfortably on the fringe.

- Experiment with the number of beads you string. Short stacks will stand up along an edge like a spiky hair-do; long floppy stacks might remind you of sea grass moving with the ocean's currents.
- Experiment with the size and weight of the beads you string—play with the proportion of the fringe to the finished piece.

Branch Fringe

Branch fringe is fun to make and has lots of possibilities—vary the fullness and length of the branches, or vary the sizes and colors of beads. For example, made in primary colors with sparse branches, branch fringe has a funny, quirky appearance. A clump of branch fringe made in brown and green beads might look like seaweed or Spanish moss.

To make branch fringe, knot your thread and come up through the fabric. String enough beads for the entire length of your fringe. Skip the last bead strung and go back through 3–5 beads of the trunk of the fringe. To make the first branch, add 3 or 4 more beads, skip the last of these beads, go back through the branch and back up 3 or 4 more beads of the trunk. At this point, and after each branch you add, it's important to adjust your tension. Hold the end bead of that branch and pull it tight, the same way you did when making basic fringe. Con-

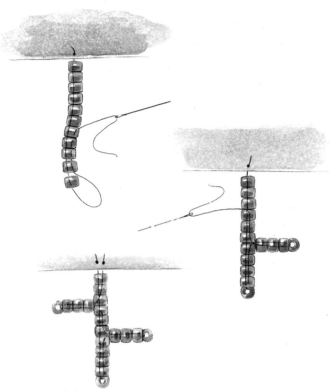

tinue adding branches all the way back to the top. Then go through the fabric and knot off on the back side.

To make the fringe fuller, add sub-branches to each branch as you work your way back up the trunk. Remember to adjust the tension after each additional branch or sub-branch.

Couching down Branch Fringe

By couching down a long snaking line of branch fringe, you can fill large areas and create a grassy texture. Knot your thread and come up through the fabric. Make a long line of branch fringe. After knot-

ting off on the underside of the fabric, determine the path you'd like your fringe to take, and couch the trunk down every 4 or 5 beads (see page 33 for couching instructions). Branches may be couched down or left to protrude for surface texture.

- Experiment with different sizes of beads. Use large beads for the trunk and small beads for the branches to create a tree-like effect, or use small beads for the trunk and large beads for the branches to create a leaf-and-stem effect.
- Vary the length of each branch to add variety to your fringe.
- Play with color gradation—vary the colors along the stems and the branches or from the top to the bottom of the whole fringe.

Picot Edging

Picot edging creates a playful frame of little points around a finished piece and works really well for sewing two pieces of fabric together at the edge. To practice the picot edge stitch, make a fold

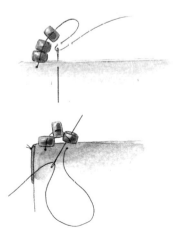

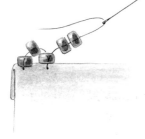

picot edging with two beads　　　**picot edging with three beads**

amount of care as you do when you're beading it. Use materials and techniques that are equal to the materials and techniques you've used to make it. Follow through with quality and care throughout the entire piece—it will be worth the time and effort.

Adding Inner Strength

To add a little rigidity to your work, trace its outside shape on a piece of high-quality quilter's plastic template, and cut it out a little inside the lines so that it fits inside of the parameters. Place the template between your work and the backing cloth and sew the two parts together. If you find you need more rigidity than one piece of template provides, cut two or more.

Using Edgings to Sew on a Backing Cloth

Trim away the extra fabric, leaving a ½-inch seam allowance around your beaded shape. Tear away the extra paper from the seam allowance. Fold the seam allowance to the back side and press with your fingers. The oil and heat from your fingers will act like an iron and press the fold into place. Otherwise, using an iron at the appropriate setting for the fabric, quickly press the folds into place (see page 23). Take care with your beads—

in your fabric. Secure your thread on the underside of the fold and come through the fold to the surface of the fabric. String 3 beads, and *at about the distance of one bead from where you started, sew across the folded edge of your fabric from the back to the front. Without piercing the fabric again, go up through the last bead strung and string on 2 more beads. Repeat from the *.

- To create a taller picot edge, start by stringing 5 beads and go up through the last two. Then from that point, string 3 at a time. Space the stitches about the width of one bead.
- Experiment using different sizes and colors of beads. Try using a larger bead or a different color for the point.
- Picot edging can be part of the body of a piece—make a small stitch in place of going through the fold.

FINISHING TECHNIQUES

You've spent a lot of time, creativity, and money making your beadwork. Now it's time to finish it. When you're finishing a piece, take the same

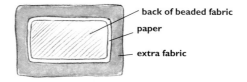

back of beaded fabric
paper
extra fabric

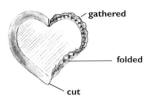

don't apply heat or pressure for too long (especially if you're using plastic beads).

Cut a piece of fabric for the backing cloth; if the backing cloth is woven fabric, leave about a ½-inch seam allowance so that you can fold the edges under. Pin the backing cloth in place. With small

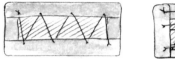

Basting the seam allowance down.

pieces, you may be able to simply hold it in place without pinning. If pinning the layers of fabric together is causing the piece to buckle, you may want to baste the folded seam allowance in place.

- If you are using felt or Ultrasuede®, you don't need to fold the edges under because they won't unravel.
- If your piece has curves, you'll need to make small cuts and folds to help the fabric fold around the curves. For inside curves, make little clips in the seam allowance almost to the fold. For outside curves, sew around the curve with tiny running stitches about ¼ inch from the edge, and pull the thread to gather the curve inward.

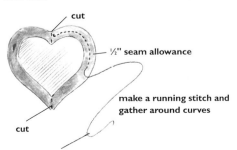

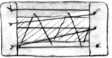

- If you can, use a thread that blends with the fabric. If the two fabrics you are binding are contrasting values or colors, match the fabric that will be most visible.
- Stitch the backing to your bead embroidery using a small whipstitch or an edging stitch like picot, buttonhole, or single stacked. Be sure to catch the edges of both the piece and the backing material in each stitch.
- If you've placed a quilting template between the layers for rigidity, it should be just a little bit smaller than the beaded piece so that you don't have to sew through the template when you're adding the backing cloth.

Making Hinges and Closures

Use the buttonhole stitch (without beads) to create hinges as well as loops for loop-and-bead closures. To make a hinge, mark where you want the hinge to attach on both pieces with a pin or light pencil mark. Decide how much space you'll need between the two parts so that they can close easily. Stitch several times between the two marks, looping the thread so that it is several threads thick. Secure the thread in the fabric and begin covering the exposed thread with buttonhole stitch. As you make each buttonhole stitch, pack the stitches close together so they cover up the exposed thread.

Making a loop-and-bead closure is similar to making a hinge. Choose a bead for your closure

and stitch it down in the spot you've chosen. Mark where you'd like the loop to be and stitch a loop that is large enough to go over the bead easily. Make the loop several threads thick, secure the thread, and cover the exposed thread with buttonhole stitch.

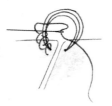

Attaching Pin and Barrette Backs

Although you can whipstitch a pin back or barrette to the back of your beaded piece, some beaders find whipstitching them awkward. I've found it faster and tidier to stitch a little fabric flap out of the same backing material, slip the bottom part of

the fastener under the flap, and then stitch down the other side of the flap.

Gluing a pin back or barrette will compromise the quality of the beadwork because, unless the glue is of archival quality, it will yellow, stain, and even rot the fabric as it ages. Also, many glues dry and fail to hold over time.

Mounting and Framing

Bead embroidery looks very nice when framed, yet it is important that the frame is not too bold or heavy. The frame should enhance your work, not attract attention to itself. When you frame your bead embroidery, either with bead stitches or an actual frame, keep in mind that the purpose of a frame is to protect the piece as well as define a space for it in a larger environment.

Use acid-free materials when framing your pieces to ensure that they'll stand the test of time. Framing materials that contain acid, such as mat board, foam core, cardboard, tape, and glue, will discolor and possibly stain your piece, or worse, cause your fabric to rot over time. For the same reasons, we recommend stitching your piece to a mounting board rather than gluing it. ✆

PROJECTS

HERE ARE TEN BEAD EMBROIDERY projects ranging from very simple to more complex. You may follow these instructions or simply use them as a springboard for your own creative adventures.

page 52

page 55

page 78

EMBELLISHED JEAN JACKET POCKET

THIS IS A QUICK AND EASY project—really! Dress up your favorite jean jacket, or any garment for that matter! In fact, you could embellish every item in your closet with fringe and other simple bead embroidery stitches. Just one garment and an hour a day, and in a short amount of time (relatively speaking, of course) you could have a completely bead-embellished wardrobe! (See the section on laundering bead embroidery, page 22.)

Knot your thread and come up through the back of the pocket flap and out the flap along the edge. String 2 size 8° seed beads and between 5 and 8 size 11° seed beads and one teardrop. Skip the teardrop and pass back through the beads and into the fabric. Knot off. Knot your thread and come out a bead's width from your first fringe. String 1 size 8° seed bead and between 4 and 7 size 11° seed beads, skip the last one, and pass back through the beads and into the fabric. Knot off and repeat across the pocket flap.

Vary the number of beads you string each time to add variation. Use a palette of similar colors of beads and mix them randomly to add visual interest. From a distance, the colors will blend together, but up close they will have extra depth.

Supplies

Materials

Seed beads, size 11° and size 8°

Teardrop beads, size 8°

Embroidery floss

Jean Jacket

Notions

Scissors

Size 10 beading needle

WINDING PATH CHOKER

Supplies

Materials

Seed beads and bugle beads, size 11°

Size D Nymo thread

Silk fabric, 3 × 24 inches

Acid-free interleaving paper, 1½ inches wide × the circumference of your neck plus 1 inch

2 sew-on snaps

Notions

Scissors   Sewing needle

Measuring tape   Pencil

Beading needle

A SIMPLE CHOKER like this one can make you feel dressed up on any occasion. The design is versatile, too—you can adapt this pattern to make a bracelet, a strap for a bag, or even a bookmark. I designed it because I love making lazy stitch pathways with undulating and meandering lines.

Measure the circumference of your neck, add 1 inch, and cut the acid-free interleaving paper to that length (it should be 1½ inches wide). Draw a meandering path on the interleaving paper. Cut the silk fabric so that it is 3½ inches wide and 2 inches longer than the circumference of your neck. Center the interleaving paper on the underside of the silk fabric and baste it in place. Use a different color of thread from the thread you'll bead with so that you can remove it easily after you've finished beading the choker. Also baste the meandering path.

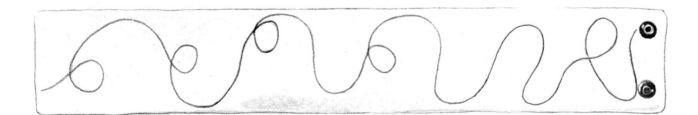

Knot your thread and work in a lazy stitch pathway (see page 29) over the length of the choker, following the meandering path you basted.

MAKING THE CHOKER

Remove the extra interleaving paper by tapping along the outside basting stitches with a moist tissue and then tearing the paper away. Remove the basting stitches. Fold ¼ inch of the length of the choker under twice on both sides and pin in place. Slip stitch to join the sides down the middle. Check the fit and mark where you want the snaps to go. You'll want it to be snug so it stays in place, but not so tight that it is uncomfortable. Fold the ends inside the choker, pin in place, and check the length again. Sew the ends closed, and then sew on the snaps. Try on the choker again, just to be sure of the fit. Finish beading to the ends of the choker.

Measure your wrist and follow the same directions to make a matching bracelet!

Slip stitch to join the sides down the middle by slipping your needle inside the fold and alternating sides.

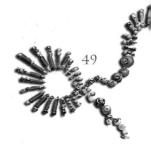

BEADED BUTTONS

THESE BUTTONS MAKE GREAT hat decorations, quilt embellishments, purse closures, pins, earrings, and collectibles, as well as serving the normal function for clothing. If you use colorfast beads (see page 15), they are washable. Once you've made a few of them, you can finish a button in less than 2 hours!

Supplies

Materials

Dritz™ Half Ball Cover Button kit (#213–45), available at most fabric stores*

Quilting-weight cotton fabric, plain or print, 3 × 3 inches

Acid-free interleaving paper (see page 20), 3 × 3 inches

Seed beads, sizes 15° to 6°, 5–8 different colors

Small charm or accent beads, optional

Nymo D beading thread in a neutral color (see page 19)

Be sure to get the domed type, not the ones that are flat on top. Also be sure to get the type that snaps closed when you pinch it with your fingers, not the type that requires a tool.

Notions	
Scissors	Sharp pencil
Beading needle	Sewing pins

These directions are for a size 45 button, which is 1¼ inches in diameter. Dritz™ makes the forms in several sizes, all of which you can adapt to these directions.

Prepare your fabric for beading by pinning the paper to the wrong side of the fabric. Cut out the guide for a size 45 button from the back of the Dritz™ package, place it in the center of the paper, and draw around it. Cut out the guide for a size 24 button, place it in the center of your previously drawn circle, and draw around the smaller guide. Baste around the smaller circle with tiny stitches through both the paper and fabric. Use a thread

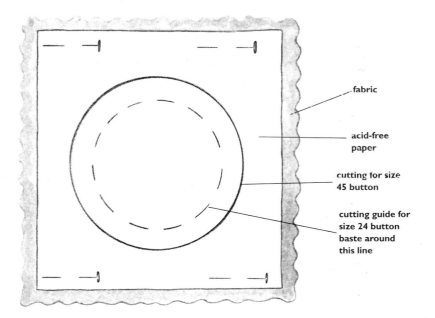

fabric

acid-free paper

cutting for size 45 button

cutting guide for size 24 button baste around this line

color that contrasts with the fabric, because your stitches will be your beading guide on the right (fabric) side.

Using Nymo D (or a beading thread of your choice), embroider your design through both paper and fabric in the area inside the smaller circle. Work just to the line of basting stitches, but not over it. The beaded surface of the button doesn't have to be flat for most purposes, so you can experiment with little stacks and larger beads.

☙ This is a great opportunity to play with the stitches and variations shown in the Techniques chapter, making a small sampler of the stitches without any pre-planning.

☙ Select a printed fabric that you like and place the inside circle so that it captures a nice part of the design. Follow the pattern on the fabric for your bead embroidery.

☙ Draw a simple design on the paper inside the inner circle. Baste along the lines of your drawing with tiny stitches to make a beading guide on the fabric side.

When your bead embroidery is complete, cut around the larger circle, cutting both paper and fabric. Moisten a tissue and tap gently around the outer edges of the inside circle on the paper side. Moistening the paper makes it tear easily. Tear away the paper border, leaving only cloth in the outer ring. The paper will remain under your beading stitches.

Sew a circle of small basting stitches around the circumference of the fabric, just ⅛ inch from the outside edge. Pull on the thread to gather the stitches and form a "puff." Your beadwork must be on the outside of the puff and the paper on the inside. Hold onto the button shank and insert the button form into the puff. Pull on the thread again to snug the gathering stitches; pull the beadwork tight over the top of the form. Knot off, keeping the tension snug. Adjust the placement of the form to make sure your beadwork is centered and smooth. Turn the button over and tuck the gathered fabric into the teeth of the form. Snap the button back in place by pinching with your fingers. You may have to push it against the edge of a table to make it snap tight.

☙ To make a circular pin, follow the above directions, except before snapping the button back in place, use a pair of pliers to squeeze and remove the shank. Sew a cloth or Ultrasuede® backing to the fabric around the edge of the button (covering the metal button back), and attach a pin back (see page 42).

☙ Make post earrings using one of the smaller Dritz™ Half Ball Cover Button kits. Remove the shank as above, glue an earring post to the metal button back, poke the post through a cloth backing, and stitch the backing to the fabric around the edge of the button (covering the metal button back, see page 42).

LEAF COIN PURSE

COUNTED CROSS-STITCH with beads creates an appealing texture and beautiful fabric. I designed this pattern by drawing an image of a leaf on graph paper. Each square in the graph paper corresponded to a stitch. It was fun to draw a freeform image of a leaf—curving and organic—then watch as it was translated into the grid that cross-stitch

creates. Because there were already so many balanced opposites in this piece (the matte thread vs. the shiny beads, the organic shape of the leave vs. the grid of the cross stitch), I decided to hint at night and day with the background. Now I have a special bag to carry ordinary objects and bring a little bead magic to my daily life.

Supplies

Materials

Seed beads, size 11° in shades of purple, blue, green, yellow, and orange (silver-lined and matte transparent)

Ivory Hardanger cloth, 22 count, 12 × 12 inches

Cotton quilting fabric (1 piece for the back, 4½ × 5½ inches; 1 piece for the lining, 5½ × 9 inches)

1 six-inch nylon zipper (match the color to the quilting fabric)

Sewing thread to match the quilting fabric

Embroidery floss, medium blue, olive green, pale green, forest green, pale yellow

Notions

8-inch embroidery hoop (with cloth wrapped around the inner ring—see page 20)

Scissors

Size 10 beading needle

Sewing needle

Straight pins

Fabric pencil

PREPARING THE FABRIC FOR BEADING

Launder all the cloth to pre-shrink the fabric. Mark the outside rectangle and the outline of the

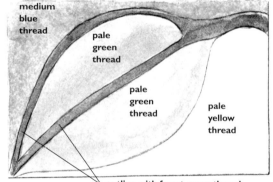

medium blue thread

pale green thread

pale green thread

pale yellow thread

outline with forest green thread

leaf on one side of the Hardanger cloth with the fabric pencil, centering the design on the fabric.

Center and secure the Hardanger cloth in the embroidery hoop. Embroidery floss contains six individual threads; cut a 20-inch length (or the distance from your fingers to your elbow) and divide it into 3 bundles of 2 strands each. Thread

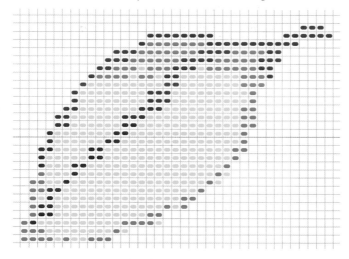

four holes square for each cross stitch

2 strands through the beading needle and knot the long end. With the pale green embroidery floss, stitch the outline of the rectangle and leaf using a running stitch. Make each stitch the length of a cross stitch—this will make counting stitches easier as you're beading.

Follow the chart to bead the leaf design in cross-stitch (see page 28). Start with the yellow section and use the yellow thread. Change to the blue thread and work the blue section, then change to the pale green thread and work the leaf.

With the forest green embroidery floss, use a running stitch to outline the left edge of the leaf as well as the center stem.

SEWING THE COIN PURSE

Trim the Hardanger cloth around the rectangle leaving a ½-inch seam allowance. Fold the top edge down along the embroidered stitches so that hardly any of the fabric is visible. Pin it along the edge of the zipper with the zipper pull closed and lined up with the right edge of the design. Using a sewing thread and needle, hand stitch the Hardanger cloth to the zipper with a slip stitch. Hand sew the outside fabric to the other side of the zipper in the same way. Fold under the seam allowance on the remaining sides of the Hardanger cloth and the quilting cloth back. Slip stitch around the outside edge of the purse. Knot off. Bury and trim the thread.

Fold the lining fabric in half, with the right side facing in, so that it measures 5½ by 4½ inches. Sew the sides up along the ½-inch seam allowance and leave the top open. Fold the top seam allowance to the outside (wrong side of fabric) so that the lining bag measures 3½ inches. Place it inside the coin purse and slip stitch it to the inside of the zipper tape. Knot off. Bury and trim the thread. Now, fill it up with coins and visit your local bead shop!

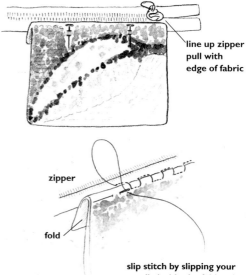

line up zipper pull with edge of fabric

zipper

fold

slip stitch by slipping your needle inside the fold and alternating sides

AMULET BAG

THIS LITTLE BAG is designed to hold a small treasure or special amulet. You can add a necklace and wear it or keep it as a pocket bag. The feminine shape is attractive with or without loopy fringe embellishments. You may follow the beading design and instructions exactly as shown in the sample, or make changes to suit your own taste.

I made the pattern for this bag by folding a sheet of paper in half and cutting shapes until I got one I liked. In the same way, you can design your own pattern if you'd like a larger bag or one with a different shape. To use the pattern shown, place your acid-free paper over the pattern (on page 58) and trace both shapes, end to end, leaving an inch of space between them.

Place the back side of the paper against the wrong side of the fabric and baste them together ½ inch from the edge. Following your traced lines of the bag front and back, make tiny running stitches through both the paper and fabric. Use a thread color that contrasts with the fabric, because these stitches will be your beading guide on the right (fabric) side. Include the fold line (back) and the flap line (front).

Supplies

Materials

Quilting-weight cotton fabric, plain or print, 4 × 8 inches

Acid-free interleaving paper (see page 20), 4 × 8 inches

Ultrasuede®, 3 × 6 inches, color of your choice for the lining

Seed beads, size 15°, 7 colors, as per the sample, about two teaspoons of each

Seed beads, size 8°, matte metallic gold color, about one teaspoon

Short bugle beads, blue, about one teaspoon

Small accent beads for loop fringe and necklace (optional)

Nymo D beading thread in a neutral color (see page 19)

Notions

Small snap, available at fabric stores	Beading needle
Scissors	Sharp pencil

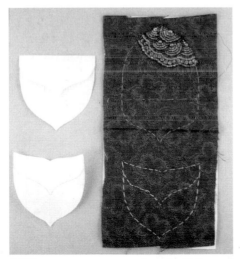

Photo by Robin Atkins

paper pattern　　　　**basted guidelines and beginning beading**

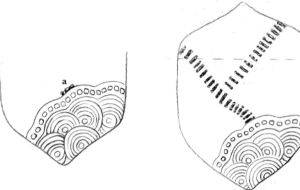

Begin working on the larger of the two bag parts, the back side and flap. Using single stitch (see page 24), sew a size 8° metallic bead just inside the stitch line about ½ inch to the right of the bottom point. Using couching stitch (see page 33), sew 5 successive rows (each a different color) of size 15° seed beads around the metallic bead, taking care not to go outside the stitch guideline. I call this "making a fan." Sew another size 8° metallic bead near the point next to the outside row of your first fan. Make a 5-row fan around this bead. Placing a size 8° metallic bead where the two fans meet, make a third fan. Make a 4th and 5th fan to fill the entire point area.

Using back stitch (see page 31), highlight this area with a line of contrasting-color size 15° seed beads (orange). Following the same line, make a little row of stacks (see page 27) with the size 8° metallic beads on the bottom and size 15° beads (any color you like) for the top or anchor beads. Highlight the beaded area again with a backstitched line of small beads.

Beginning at point *a*, make a pathway with small bugle beads and a matching color size 15° seed bead on each end (see page 30). Just before the fold line for the flap, split the path as shown. Highlight the path with a line of contrasting-color size 15° beads (orange) on one side and a different color on the other side. Make a line of stacks along the side of the path with the orange highlight, then another line of back stitched beads. Fill the areas along the path and at the "y" in the path

with more fans. Use concentric back stitched lines of size 15° seed beads to fill the remaining areas of the piece.

Begin the front of the bag the same way as the back, making a fan shape ½ inch to the right of the bottom point. Continue making fans, a highlight line, a line of stacks, a pathway, and concentric lines of fill to complete the front of the bag. Do not sew beads in the area that will be under the flap when the bag is closed.

ASSEMBLING THE BAG

When your bead embroidery is complete, you're ready to line the front and back pieces and join them. First moisten a tissue and use it to tap gently around the paper at the outer edges of both the bag front and back. Carefully tear away the extra paper so only the cloth remains, except for the paper under your beading stitches and where the flap will close. Cut the two pieces apart. Cut around each piece, leaving a ½-inch seam

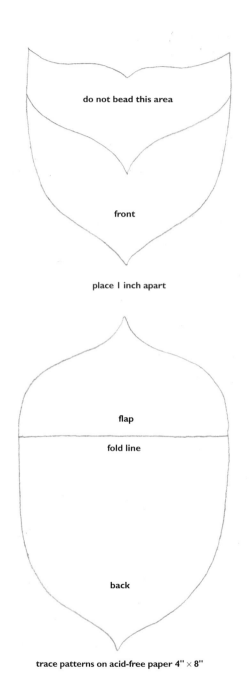

do not bead this area

front

place 1 inch apart

flap

fold line

back

trace patterns on acid-free paper 4" × 8"

allowance. Clip the seam allowance at the top center of the bag front, being careful not to clip farther than the stitch outline guide. Fold in the seam allowance and finger press (see page 40). If it doesn't stay in place, baste it down with large temporary stitches.

Trace the pattern for both the front and back pieces on plain paper. Cut out the shapes and use them as patterns to cut the lining pieces from Ultrasuede®. Using tiny whipstitches in a thread color that matches the lining, sew the lining pieces . to the bag pieces, covering the paper and folded seam allowances. Sew the "outie" snap part to the lining of the flap near the point. Sew the "innie" snap part to the bag front, placing it so the flap will be aligned correctly when the bag is closed.

Now that both the front and back pieces are lined and complete, sew them together using size 15° beads and the picot edge stitch (see page 39). Be sure that you catch a little fabric from both the front and back with each stitch. Continue the picot edge stitch all the way around the flap.

If you like, you can further embellish the bag in any way you want. Add a small dagger-shaped accent bead to the point of the flap to make it easier to open and close. Add a necklace, attaching one end to each side of the bag by sewing through and knotting off inside. Add loopy fringe to the bottom of the bag and the sides where the necklace is attached. Use dagger-shaped beads in the center of each loop.

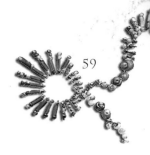

SPIRAL HEART PIN

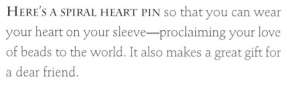

HERE'S A SPIRAL HEART PIN so that you can wear your heart on your sleeve—proclaiming your love of beads to the world. It also makes a great gift for a dear friend.

The trick to this technique is matching the colors in the design with beads. Although size 15° and size 11° beads are available in many colors, there isn't a bead for every color that occurs in the world. So, as an artist mixes paint, you must mix your beads to get the color you need. Up close, the beads will keep their individual color, but when they are viewed from a distance they will appear mixed, like a pointillist painting or a mosaic.

Step away from your pin occasionally and look at it from a distance—what seemed unintelligible close up may come into focus from a distance. I also find that a design may not come together until the very end, so I continue beading on faith, hoping it will all come together when I've completed the piece. It usually does!

BEADING THE PIN

Color photocopy or scan and print the image to the right onto acid-free typing paper or draw your own design. Cut out the design to the edge of the image, center, and stitch the paper to the right side of the fabric.

Knot your thread, come up in the center of the design, and work in back stitch in a continuous

Supplies

Materials

Seed beads, size 15°, an assortment of reds, purples, oranges, and yellows of different values, hues, and surfaces

Size D Nymo, white (see page 19)

Cotton quilting fabric, 6 × 6 inches

Acid-free typing paper [1]

Heat-resistant quilting template, 2 × 3 inches

Ultrasuede®, 2 × 3 inches

¾-inch pin back

[1] Acid-free typing paper is available at most office supply shops.

Notions

Scissors

Size 11 sharp needle

Pen or pencil

Permission is granted to copy this design for personal use.

spiraling line. Start with 2 beads, stitch them to the fabric, and go back through both beads; string 2 more, stitch them to the fabric, go through both beads again, and string 2 more. Once your circle is started, proceed with back stitch normally (see

page 31). When you reach the edge of the design, turn back and work the other direction until you fill the area.

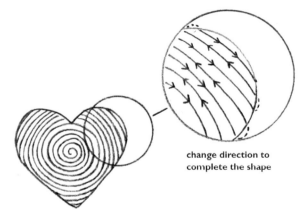

change direction to complete the shape

Use the paper design as a cartoon[2] and choose beads that match the color on the paper as you bead the piece. Completely cover the paper with beads.

After you've finished beading, cut away the extra fabric around the heart, leaving a ½-inch seam allowance. Clip almost to the seam line at the top center of the heart. Starting just to one side of the clip, baste a running stitch around the edge of the heart to the other side of the clip on the seam allowance (see page 41).

Trace the outline of the heart on the quilting template and cut it out. Use the template to cut a piece of Ultrasuede® for the backing. Place the quilting template against the underside of the fabric and cinch the basting thread around the template until it is snug. Knot off. Whipstitch across the lower half of the heart to pull the sides in and keep the quilting template in place.

Stitch the Ultrasuede® to the beaded fabric along the edge using an edging stitch like picot or stacked single stitch (see page 27 or 39).

ATTACHING THE PIN BACK

Cut a ½-inch square piece of Ultrasuede® and whipstitch it to the back of the heart. Insert the bottom half of the pin back under the flap and whipstitch it securely in place. Now pin your heart over your heart and show the world what you have to offer.

[2] *Cartoon is a weaving term—it is a drawing that is used as a guide for creating a design.*

SNAKE/HEART NEEDLECASE

Supplies

Materials

Seed beads, size 15°, 11°, 8°, 6°, and 4° (select a mixture of silver-lined size 11° and matte transparent seed beads of a similar value and hue for the lazy stitch background)

One ¾-inch oval lampwork bead

Bugle beads, size 11°

Size D Nymo thread (see page 19)

Cotton quilting fabric, 6 × 6 inches

Acid-free interleaving paper (see page 20), 6 × 6 inches

Heat-resistant quilting template, one 8½ × 11 inch sheet

Felt, 8 × 11 inches

Ultrasuede®, 6 × 6 inches

Sewing thread to match the felt and Ultrasuede®

Embroidery floss

Notions	
	Embroidery needle
Scissors	
	Pen or pencil
Size 11 needle	
	4 straight pins

I STARTED THIS NEEDLECASE in an improvisational bead embroidery class that Robin taught. I chose a snake inside a heart as the image for this piece for its multi-layered symbolism. I see the snake as a symbol for transformation (among other things) because it sheds its skin; the heart is a universal symbol for love—the heart is also as the container for the soul. I beaded meandering pathways through the heart and around the snake. They are journeys of self-discovery.

GETTING STARTED

Trace the design on page 64 on the acid free interleaving paper. Center and stitch the interleaving paper to the underside of the fabric. With a thread color that you can see easily on the right side of the fabric, stitch along the outlines of the design with a small running stitch to define your beading areas.

MAKING THE SNAKE

Make the snake first, starting with the head. Knot your thread and come up at point *a*. String a size 6° bead, the large lampwork bead, and another size 6° bead, and sew them in place securely by stitching through the beads several times. Knot off. Start couching (see page 33) around the head, following the outline for the snake body, using size 11° seed beads. Gradually transition from a dark color to a light color and back again throughout the body of the snake. Add a size 6° bead every 3 rows of couching to couch around (Robin calls this technique "making fans"). As

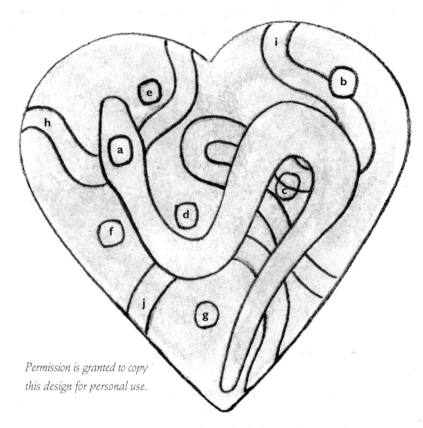

Permission is granted to copy this design for personal use.

size 11° and 2 size 15° beads. Knot off after each barnacle dot. Make barnacle dots at points *c*–*g*.

MAKING BUGLE BEAD PATHWAYS

Starting at point *h*, make bugle bead pathways (see page 30) through the heart, following the lines that you basted on the piece. Make sure to string a size 15° bead before and after each bugle bead to protect the thread from the bugle bead's sharp edges. Fill in areas on the pathway that are too narrow for the bugle beads with size 11° seed beads of a similar color. Knot off when you end and start the path again as the pathway meanders under the snake and the barnacle dots.

FILLING IN AROUND THE SNAKE AND PATHWAYS

Use lazy stitch (see page 29) to fill in between the snake and pathways. Alternate sections of silver-lined beads with matte transparent beads of a similar value and hue. This slight variation in surface as well as size will create depth and add a more subtle pathway for your eye to travel through the piece.

MAKING THE NEEDLECASE

Turn the piece over (beaded side down) and trace the outside shape of the heart on the quilting template. Use your actual piece for this, instead of the pattern in the book, so that it is the exact shape of the piece. Cut 4 hearts out of the quilting template. Use the template to cut out 4 pieces of felt for the inside of the needlecase.

you near the tail of the snake and the space gets smaller, transition to smaller beads to couch around so that the tail tapers nicely to the end. Knot off and cut your thread.

MAKING THE BARNACLE DOTS

Knot your thread and come up at point *b* to make the barnacle dots that punctuate this piece. Make a single-stack stitch with a size 4° bead, a size 11° bead, and a size 15° bead. Surround the stacked stitch with a barnacle (see page 27) using

*Cut away the extra fabric around the beaded heart, leaving a ½-inch seam allowance. Clip almost to the seam line at the top center of the heart. Starting just to one side of the clip, baste a running stitch around the edge of the heart to the other side of the clip on the seam allowance (see page 41). Place two of the heart-shaped quilting templates against the underside of the fabric and gather the basting thread around the template until it is snug. Knot off. Whipstitch across the lower half of the heart to pull the sides in and keep the quilting template in place.

Trim ¹⁄₁₆ inch off one of the heart-shaped pieces of felt. This slightly smaller felt heart will provide extra padding for the needlecase. Lay it over the quilting template, followed by the slightly larger heart-shaped felt. Stitch the top layer of felt to the beaded fabric along the edge using a stacked single stitch with a size 8° and a size 11° seed bead.

To make the second part of the heart-shaped needlecase, trace the heart shape with the quilting template on the underside of the Ultrasuede®. Repeat from the *, except use the picot stitch (see page 39) with 1 size 6° and 2 size 8° beads.

MAKING HINGES AND A BEAD-AND-LOOP CLOSURE

Lay the front and the back pieces of the needlecase right side down, side by side on a table. Mark the location of the hinges with the straight pins on either side. Cut an 18-inch length of embroidery floss and separate the strands into 3 groups of 2. Using 2 strands of embroidery floss and an embroidery needle, knot the thread and bury the knot in the seam. Loop between points *a* and *b* 3 times. You want the loops to be loose enough so that you can close the needlecase easily, but not so

loose that the hinge sticks out a lot when the case is closed. Cover the loops with tiny buttonhole stitches (without beads—see page 41) and knot off. Make hinges at points *c* and *d* and at points *e* and *f*.

Mark the location of the bead-and-loop closure with the straight pins at points *g* and *h*. At point *h*, make a stem for your bead by looping through the bead 2 times; cover the stem with buttonhole stitches like the hinges. Knot off and bury the thread in the needlecase and trim the thread. At point *g*, make the loop (see page 42). Test the loop to make sure it fits over the bead easily. Cover it with buttonhole stitches and knot off and bury the thread before cutting it off. Now place your needle in your new needlecase!

LARGE DRAWSTRING BAG

Supplies

Materials

½ yard quilting-weight cotton fabric for the beaded center panel and bag lining (Fabric A)

½ yard pre-quilted sand-washed rayon or silk for the bag [1] (Fabric B)

8 pieces color-coordinated fabrics (cotton, rayon, or silk), cut as follows:

Blue/purple print no. 1, 2¼ inches × 5¾ inches

Blue/purple print no. 1, 2¼ inches × 6½ inches

Red/fuchsia print no. 2, 2¼ inches × 5¾ inches

Red/fuchsia print no. 2, 2¼ inches × 6½ inches

Blue/purple print no. 3, 2¼ inches × 8¼ inches

Blue/purple print no. 3, 2¼ inches × 9 inches

Red/fuchsia print no. 4, 2¼ inches × 8¼ inches

Red/fuchsia print no. 4, 2¼ inches × 9 inches

Acid-free interleaving paper (see page 20), 5 × 6 inches

Seed beads, size 11°, 9 colors, as per the sample, about one tablespoon of each

Small accent beads—bronze leaves and antique nailheads (or faceted round beads)

Sequins—small round bronze sequins and large white-opal star sequins (optional)

Large shell button, about ⅞ inch in diameter

3 small silver star charms

3 small bells and 3 star charms for the ends of the drawstrings

Selection of color-coordinated yarns and decorative cords for drawstrings

Nymo D beading thread in a neutral color (see page 19)

[1] Pre-quilted cotton will also work for the bag.

Notions

Scissors	Sewing pins
Beading needle	Large safety pin
Sharp pencil	

USE THIS LARGE DRAWSTRING BAG to protect a treasured book or hold your special lingerie when traveling. Add a strap and carry it as a purse, or stuff it like a decorative pillow and tuck it in a corner where you can admire it frequently. Although this bag is large (12 inches wide by 14 inches high), it doesn't take long to make because only the small center panel is beaded solidly.

The color scheme for this bag includes all the rich jewel tones: teal, purple, ruby, fuchsia, and periwinkle, plus gold, bronze, and silver. I was influenced toward these colors by the fabric I selected for beading the center panel, which is also the lining fabric. It is a bright, jewel-tone and metallic-gold paisley print in 100 percent cotton.

When I begin a project, I generally do not have a plan for the outcome, nor do I draw a design for the bead embroidery. I simply start by sewing on a bead or a button that appeals to me and go from there. The beading fabric always influences my work—its colors, scale, personality, and flow.

In making this bag, you have several design choices. With bead colors and fabrics similar to those in my example, you can follow the directions below and use my design as a model. Or you can choose one of the following options:

- You can approach this project in the improvisational way described above, selecting any fabric for the beadwork that appeals to you and allowing it to influence your work.
- You can draw your own design (see page 83).
- You can find a fabric that appeals to you and bead the design that is printed on the fabric.

BEADING THE CENTER

Draw a rectangle 4¼ by 3¾ inches on a sheet of acid-free paper. Measure and draw a ½-inch border around all sides of the rectangle. Cut out the paper along this outside rectangle (5¼ by 4¾ inches). Cut a piece of fabric A the same size. Place the back side of the paper against the wrong side of the fabric and pin them together. Following the lines of the inner rectangle drawn on the paper, make small running stitches through both the paper and fabric. Use a thread color that contrasts with the fabric, because these stitches will be your beading guide on the right (fabric) side.

Make the border first. Using back stitch (see page 31), sew a line of periwinkle-color beads around the perimeter of the beading area. Follow the line of your basting stitches. Sew a second line of beads inside the first. Using lazy stitch (see page 29) with three beads per stitch, sew lines of beads inside and perpendicular to the periwinkle perimeter. Use three colors to create a twisted ribbon effect. Sew another line of periwinkle beads just inside the lazy stitches to complete the border.

lazy stitch pattern repeat these 12 rows

back stitch lines of outside border

Sew a large button slightly above and to the left of center. Sew several times through the holes of the button as you would for a garment so that it's firmly attached. Knot off on the back. Then sew through one hole again, add a few beads, and sew back down through the other hole to cover your thread stitches. Knot off on the back again.

Using back stitch, sew a line of red beads in a long, backward "S" shape diagonally from the top left hand corner to the lower right. You can do this freehand or draw the line on the back, baste it, and follow your basting stitches. Make two more lines of red beads along the first. Still using back stitch, outline this S-shaped area with lines of bronze

beads. Think of the button as a "sun," and make more radiating lines of bronze beads curving out from it. On the left side, bring your lines all the way to the border. On the right, make shorter lines.

Sew bronze leaf-shaped beads around the button between the lines of bronze beads. To the left of the S path, use faceted bronze beads to back stitch spirals radiating out from the leaves. For the center of each spiral, use an antique nailhead bead or any round, faceted bronze bead. Fill the area between the spirals and lines with single stitch (see page 24) and stacked single stitch (see page 27). Note that this area is largely red, fuchsia, and gold. The left side of the panel is now complete.

Next, make the three "moons." Using silver beads, back stitch three crescent-shaped lines in the upper right corner. For each "moon," back stitch a second line of silver beads inside and snug against the crescent, but don't bead the second line all the way to the tip. In the "ditch" between the two lines

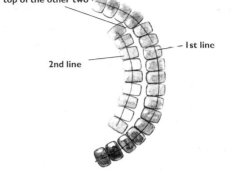

3rd line starts here and rests on top of the other two

2nd line

— 1st line

of beads, back stitch a third, raised line. This line gives the "moons" some dimension. Using back stitch and couching (see pages 31–33), fill the remaining areas of the panel. Note that this area is largely green, teal, and purple. Make a short fringe (see page 37) from the bottom of each "moon," adding a silver star charm at the end of each fringe.

ADDING THE FABRIC BORDER

Now you are ready to make the panel larger by adding borders of fabric around the beaded area. If you are familiar with quilting, you may recognize this as the log-cabin technique.

Prepare your beadwork by removing the paper from the seam allowance. Moisten a tissue and use it to tap gently around the paper at the outer edges of the beaded border. Carefully tear away the extra paper so only the cloth remains, except for the paper under your beading stitches.

Working counter-clockwise around the beaded panel, sew a border of fabric strips to the edges. Place the short no. 1 strip face-down along the right

edge of the beaded panel, lining up the top right corner of the panel with the corner of the strip. The end of the strip will hang down below the lower edge of the panel. Hand sew, using tiny running stitches, along the right side of the panel. (It's not

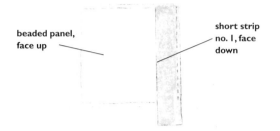

beaded panel, face up

short strip no. I, face down

possible with a sewing machine to sew the border fabric snugly against the beads, even using a zipper foot.) As you sew, feel the outside line of beads with your fingertips and try to stitch right next to them. Knot off at the end, open out the fabric strip, and finger-press the seam toward the fabric strip.

Place the long no. 1 strip face-down along the top edge of the beaded panel, lining up the top right corner of the first strip with the second strip. Hand sew, open out, and finger-press as above. Place the short no. 2 strip along the left edge of the

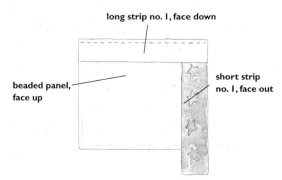

long strip no. I, face down

beaded panel, face up

short strip no. I, face out

panel, lining up the top left corners. Sew, open, and finger-press as above. Place the long no. 2 strip along the bottom edge of the panel, lining up the bottom left corners. Sew, open, and finger-press as above. Sew the inside edge of the first strip to the last strip where they overlap.

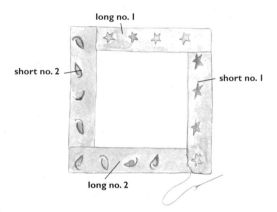

long no. I

short no. 2

short no. I

long no. 2

In the same way as above, attach the no. 3 and no. 4 strips to bring the panel to its full size of 9½ inches by 10 inches. For this second set of strips, you can stitch either by hand or by machine. The seam allowance is ½ inch. Fold under the ½-inch seam allowance along the outside edge of the completed panel and iron it in place.

FINISHING THE BAG

Cut one piece of quilted fabric B, 13 inches wide by 29 inches long, for the bag. Fold it in half, with the right side of the fabric out, to form a rectangle 13 inches wide by 14½ inches high. The fold is the bottom of the bag. Center the beaded panel on the bag 1¼ inches above the bottom fold. Pin the panel

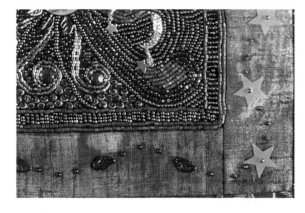

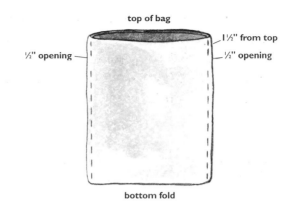

top of bag

1½" from top

½" opening   ½" opening

bottom fold

in place, taking care to pin through only the top layer of bag fabric. Baste it in place close to the outer edge. Using bronze seed beads and the picot edge stitch (see page 39), stitch the panel to the bag fabric. Be sure to catch both the bag fabric and the turned-under edge of the panel with each stitch. It may help to fold the bag fabric at the stitching line. Remove the basting stitches. Using single stitch, seed beads, bronze leaves, and star-shaped sequins, decorate the inside fabric border with a waving line. Sew through both layers—the fabric strips and bag fabric.

If you like, embellish the pre-quilted fabric of the bag with seed beads and sequins. Using single stitch, sew seed beads evenly spaced along the lines of machine quilting. Sew sequins where the machine quilting lines cross. Do not embellish the seam allowances.

To construct the bag, reverse the bottom fold so that the beadwork is inside. Using a machine (or hand-sewing with tiny running stitches) and a ½-inch seam allowance, sew the sides of the bag. Leave a ½-inch opening on each side, 1½ inches from the top, for the drawstrings. Back stitch to reinforce both the top and bottom of the opening.

Cut a piece of lining fabric A, 13 inches wide by 29 inches long. With a ½-inch seam allowance, sew the sides of the lining. Do not leave an opening in the lining seams. Leave the lining with the seams out, turn the seam allowance at the top to the outside, and press. Turn the bag right side out, turn the seam allowance top to the inside, and press. Slip the lining into the bag. Using tiny whip-

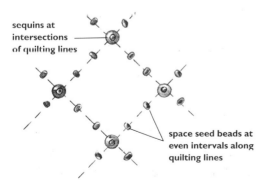

sequins at intersections of quilting lines

space seed beads at even intervals along quilting lines

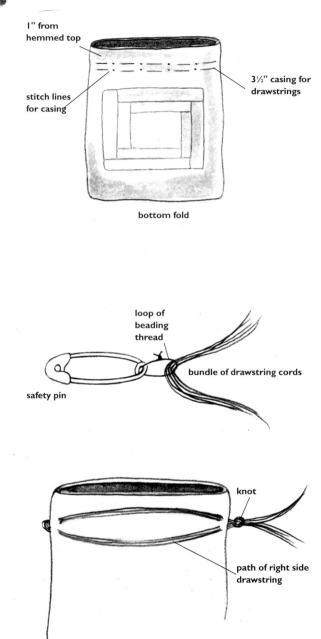

1" from
hemmed top

stitch lines
for casing

3½" casing for
drawstrings

bottom fold

loop of
beading
thread

safety pin

bundle of drawstring cords

knot

path of right side
drawstring

stitches, hand sew the top of the lining to the top of the bag. Or you might want to use the picot edge stitch to join the lining to the bag. Using a machine (or hand-sewing with tiny running stitches), sew around the top of the bag through both lining and bag fabrics to make a casing for the drawstrings.

Cut two bundles of various yarns and cords in 20-inch lengths for the drawstrings. I used predominantly reds and bronzes for one bundle, blues and bronzes for the other. Thread a 6-inch length of beading thread through the spring of a closed safety pin and knot the two ends to form a loop. Put the ends of one of the bundles through the loop. Use the safety pin to guide the bundle through the casing, starting on the right side of the bag. Pull the bundle all the way around until it comes out the same side of the bag. Even the ends of the bundle and tie them together with an overhand knot at the edge of the bag. Using the same loop-and-pin technique, work the second bundle through the same casing all the way around, starting from the other side of the bag. Even the ends and tie an overhand knot at the edge of the bag. If the threads and yarns are the type that will fray or unravel, tie an overhand knot at the end of each thread. On three of the threads on each side, tie a bell or star charm into the knots.

JOURNAL,
PHOTO ALBUM, BOOK

THIS PROJECT USES A SIMPLE photo-transfer method to print any photo on fabric, which you can then embellish with bead embroidery and use to cover a small book. For the sample, I chose a spiral-bound blank book, six inches tall, with black pages for mounting photographs. When selecting a pre-made book, look for one with removable covers, which will make it easier to attach your finished bead embroidery. Although there are many possibilities for covering books with bead embroidery, this project describes a method that doesn't require special supplies or previous bookbinding experience. For the sample shown here, I used Computer Printer Fabric™ (manufactured by June Tailor in Richfield, Wisconsin), available at some fabric and craft

Supplies

Materials

Pre-made spiral book, preferably with covers that can be removed[1]

Kit for transferring photos to fabric [2]

Photo image, about one-third the size of your book cover

Acid-free interleaving paper (see page 20), the same size as your book cover

Seed beads, sizes 15° to 6°, 5–10 colors, about ½ teaspoon per color

Seed beads, size 11°, background color (beige or pale yellow), about 2 tablespoons

Assorted flower-shaped and leaf-shaped beads (or other accent beads of your choice)

Nymo D beading thread in a neutral color (see page 19)

2 pieces of Ultrasuede®, each 2 inches larger than the book cover, in a color of your choice[3]

Acid-free book binding glue, such as PVA Adhesive[4]

Attractive paper to face the insides of the covers

Notions

Beading needle	Waxed paper
Pencil, ruler, glue brush (inexpensive 1-inch paintbrush)	Scissors
	Paper towels
Tailor's chalk	

1 Available at many art supply, craft, stationery, photo, rubber stamp, and book stores.
2 Some kits include fabric; for others you must also find appropriate fabric, as specified in the kit's directions. Kits are available at fabric, quilting, computer, and craft supply stores.
3 Available at many fabric shops and craft supply stores. I suggest finding a color that closely matches either the cover of your book or a color in your photo image.
4 Available at art supply and bookmaking shops.

shops. You can print on this paper-backed treated fabric with a laser or inkjet printer, just as you would a normal sheet of paper. After printing your photo, you simply peel off the paper backing and set the image by ironing. For other similar products, you print the picture (or take it to a place that makes color copies) on special paper, then transfer the image to a tight-weave, light-colored fabric with an iron. Because new kits for transferring images to cloth enter the market frequently, we suggest you consult your local quilting shop (or computer supply shop) for the latest and best products.

PREPARING YOUR IMAGE

On a piece of computer paper, draw around the cover of your pre-made book, centering it on the paper. Exclude the area with punched holes. Then outline the area you plan to bead, centering it within the outline of the cover. Add a ½-inch seam allowance around your designated beading area. Plan the placement of your photo within the beading area. In my sample, the beadwork area goes all the way to the top and bottom of the cover, but not to the sides. For a 6-inch square cover, I planned the bead embroidery to be 5¾ inches tall by 4¾ inches wide.

Before you print your photo on the transfer medium, practice printing it on plain paper. Check the alignment of the image by holding the printed copy and your drawing together against a window. If the alignment is not correct, consult your printer's

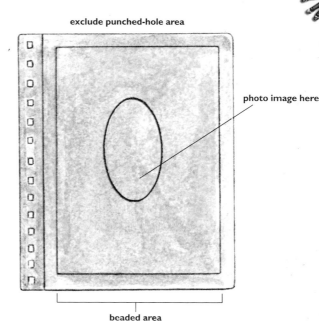

exclude punched-hole area

photo image here

beaded area

documentation to see how to fix it. When the alignment is correct, print your image according to the directions on the kit.

Prepare for beading by turning the seam allowance of the printed fabric to the back side. Cut a piece of acid-free interleaving paper slightly smaller than the beading area and baste it to the underside of the fabric, catching the turned seam allowances in your basting stitches. You are now ready to bead!

BEADING THE IMAGE

Frame the entire beading area using picot edge stitch (see page 39). Create a rainbow effect by changing the color every second picot. Next, using back stitch (see page 31), make a line of beads just

inside the picot edge stitch. Change colors as needed to continue the rainbow effect. Use back stitch to outline corner areas. Sew an attractive flower and leaf combination in each corner. Make a row of little stacks (see page 27) all around the border. Then sew another line of contrasting-colored beads inside that row.

Circle the photo image with flower-shaped and leaf-shaped accent beads, using single stitch (see page 24) to hold them in place. Now you are ready to fill in the background. On the paper side of beading, find and mark the center point of your work. Draw lines from the center point to the corners. Draw a vertical and a horizontal line through the center point to the edges of your beading area. With these lines as guides, use back stitch to create radiating lines of beads in the background color from the center garland of flowers to the border. Space these lines as evenly as you can without getting out your micrometer. Finally, fill the areas between the lines using back stitch, couching, or lazy stitch (whichever is easiest for you).

MAKING THE COVER

When your bead embroidery is complete, baste it in the center of a piece of Ultrasuede®, which was previously cut 2 inches larger than your book cover. Using a running stitch and a neutral color of thread, sew your bead embroidery to the Ultrasuede® between and under the garland of flowers. In the same way, sew between the border

and the background beads. Then, using a thread color that matches the Ultrasuede® and starting at one outside corner, tack down the point of each picot all the way around. Remove your original basting stitches.

Place your beadwork over the book cover, fold the extra Ultrasuede® around the edges of the cover, and adjust the placement until it is exactly where you want it. Carefully mark where the Ultrasuede® folds around the edges of the cover with tailor's chalk. Leaving ⅝ inch to turn to the inside of the cover, trim away the extra Ultrasuede®. Also trim away any excess Ultrasuede® from the side with the holes punched for the ring binding.

Ultrasuede® seam allowances

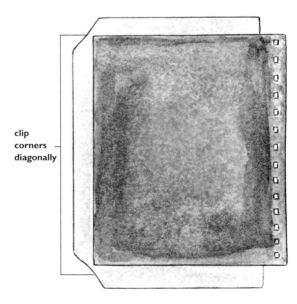

clip
corners
diagonally

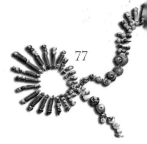

Using acid-free bookbinding glue, brush a light coating over the cover. Keep the area of the punched holes free of glue! Let the glue dry a few minutes until it feels slightly tacky to your touch. Apply your beadwork to the cover, adjusting placement as necessary. When the glue is completely dry, clip the corners of the Ultrasuede® diagonally. Apply a thin coating of glue to both the Ultrasuede® and the margins around the inside of the cover. When the glue feels tacky, fold, press, and hold the Ultrasuede® to the inside with your fingers. Turn the cover face down on a hard surface (covered with waxed paper, in case of glue seepage). Place several sheets of paper towel over your beadwork as padding, and cover it with a few heavy books or magazines. Allow the cover to dry completely (overnight).

Cut a piece of decorative paper just slightly smaller than the cover (excluding the punched-hole area). Brush it lightly with glue. Allow the glue to dry until tacky; then position it inside the cover to conceal the folded Ultrasuede® edges. Weight the cover as above, and allow it to dry completely (overnight).

You may wish to cover the back cover in the same way, using the second piece of Ultrasuede® and decorative paper.

Sashiko Vest

by Dustin Wedekind

Supplies

Materials

¾ yard top fabric

½ yard lining fabric

½ yard flannel for batting (optional)

Seed beads, size 11°, white

Assorted embellishing beads and/or nailheads[1]

Nymo D in color to match fabric (see page 19)

Quilting thread

Graph paper

---

[1] Special thanks to East of Oz for supplying the vintage nailheads (see Resources page 130).

Notions

Tape	Scissors
Sewing machine	Fabric marking pencil
Pins	Ballpoint pen
Needles	Transfer paper

SASHIKO IS A TRADITIONAL quilting art from Japan. It uses white thread on Indigo fabric to create dazzling patterns for a utilitarian purpose. The layers of fabric provide warmth, while the quilting stitches can offer symbolic protection and well-wishes for the wearer. The fabrics can be cotton, wool, or silk.

This vest form is loosely interpreted from Japanese armor. In medieval Japan, plates of metal were laced together (*odashi*) to make rectangular flaps (especially the *sodi* shoulder plates and *kusazuri* skirting) that were tied to the main suit (*dô*). The vest flaps are finished works of art in themselves. Breaking the vest into sections makes it easier to manipulate while beading. And the quilted layers allow you to bead without a hoop.

Making the Vest

Pre-wash and press your fabric. The pattern is based on 8½ by 11 inch sheets of graph paper. Using 8 sheets of paper, tape together a paper vest to try for size. Note that these pieces do not allow for a seam allowance. The bottom front panels are whole rectangles. To make the top front panels, fold the paper in half length-wise,

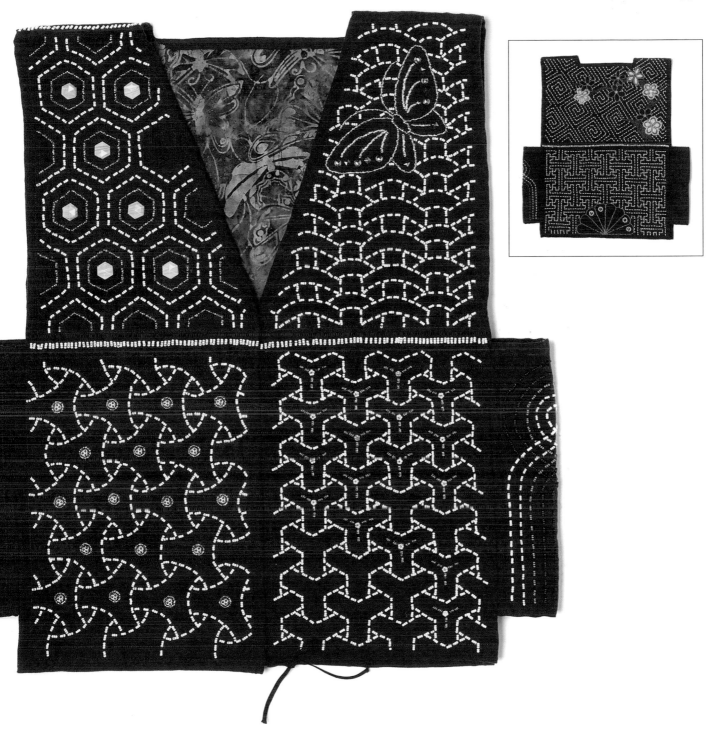

Sashiko Designs

Many books are available that show myriad sashiko designs. This vest uses six different designs, plus added elements that were beaded before and after the patterns were completed. When drawing your patterns, keep the lines between ¼ and ½ inch apart.

Inazuma, lightning, is very easy to draw and stitch. The continuous line loops back on itself to look like two lines. The plum blossom is a popular motif. Draw the flower and branch outlines and work the pattern up to those lines. Begin the flowers with a nailhead center, then back stitch the petals around it. The branch is beaded with dense lazy stitches.

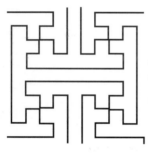

Sayagata, or silk weave, also known as monk's maze, looks very complex, but you will find that it is made of continuous lines that intersect, making it easy to stitch. The half chrysanthemum at the bottom back of vest is decorated with nailheads surrounded with freshwater pearls.

Kikko, tortoise shell, looks like a honeycomb. It is a simple pattern to follow but requires a lot of blind stitching on the back. The vest is embellished with hexagonal nailheads (a lucky find!).

Don't be timid about making up your own patterns. This basket weave is easy to draw but tricky to stitch because it doesn't have any continuous lines. The butterfly can be filled with a variety of colors and techniques to accent any part of the vest.

open the fold, and then fold at an angle from the top center to the bottom corner. The back two panels are each made of two rectangles taped together, with a notch made in the top one for the neck. Make consistent alterations to all the pieces of paper. If the overall length needs to be an inch shorter, take ½ inch off the length of each piece. The side panels are the most adjustable areas, so make these adjustments after making the vest of fabric. The vest pictured was trimmed to 8 inches wide on all pieces.

Lay the pattern pieces on the fabric. Cut the top fabric with a 1½-inch seam allowance all around. Cut the lining and batting pieces with a ⅜-inch allowance. Pin the layers of fabric, centering the lining on the top fabric. Use the marking pencil to

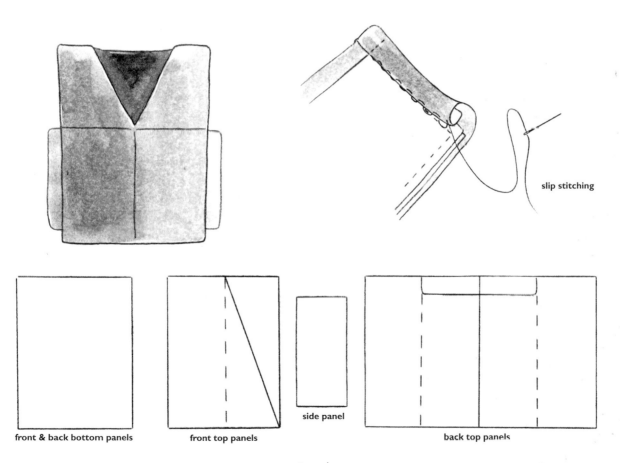

slip stitching

front & back bottom panels   front top panels   side panel   back top panels

pattern pieces

trace the outline of the rectangles. Follow this line with the sewing machine using a straight stitch.

Trim the lining and batting to an even ¼ inch from the stitching. Bind the edges by folding the top fabric to the back and slip stitching by hand to cover the machine stitching.

Use safety pins to hold the vest together and try it on for size. Measure the gap under the armpit and repeat the steps above to make two side panels. They don't need to be as long as the front and back panels and can even be tapered at the bottom to make the vest more form-fitting.

ASSEMBLING THE VEST

When you are finished beading, use quilting thread to whipstitch the panels together. Use a doubled beading thread to cover the seams with lazy stitches.

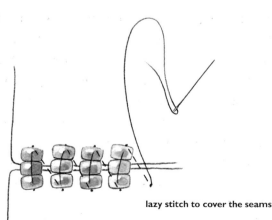

lazy stitch to cover the seams

Beading the Vest

Draw Sashiko patterns on the paper pieces. Use the transfer paper and a ballpoint pen to transfer your design to the vest.

Follow the lines with a running lazy stitch (see page 29), using three beads per stitch. Bring the needle up a bead's width from the last stitch. Secure your tail threads between the layers of fabric. Try to work the edges of the patterns first to prevent rubbing off the transferred markings.

- Make the stitches slightly longer than the beads so that they don't hump up on the fabric.
- Watch that intersecting lines don't overlap. If your next stitch overlaps a line, string two beads and then couch them down. Sometimes when you do lazy stitch with 2 beads, the beads tilt so that the holes are exposed. Couch between the 2 beads to prevent exposed holes.
- Pass your working thread between the layers of fabric to get to another line. You can work patterns with continuous lines more quickly, and most patterns are deceptively made of continuous lines, so plan your stitching path before you begin beading.
- For added bead security, knot off at each turn.
- A patterned lining fabric helps camouflage knots and erratic stitches.

DESIGNING FOR BEAD EMBROIDERY

AMY'S THOUGHTS ABOUT DESIGN

I BELIEVE THAT CREATIVITY is part of what makes us human—it is more than just creating things to protect us from the elements or to make our day-to-day survival easier. We have a desire to perceive and reflect what surrounds us—sometimes we perceive happiness, sometimes despair, sometimes beauty, sometimes ugliness. There are many ways of creating that communicate these feelings.

Learning to design also means learning to perceive. In the same way that listening goes beyond hearing, perceiving goes beyond simply seeing. It means becoming aware of your surroundings through all of your senses. Perceiving is also seeing with your heart and mind. Designing involves taking what you perceive and translating it into a visual language.

Within visual language, the tools of communication are the elements of design—line, shape, texture, pattern, and color. These elements can create moods and communicate ideas and thoughts. A soft line that travels diagonally from one corner to another may give a design a feeling of gentle movement, a warm yellow may evoke memories of sunlight on a patch of hardwood floor, or the illusion of a fuzzy texture on a rounded shape may remind you of a cat. Taken all together, simple elements create an image as well as a mood.

Use a Viewfinder to Make a Sampler

Try this exercise to help you think about how you perceive the elements of design.[1]

Find a colorful magazine that you don't mind

If You Hesitate Before Reading this Chapter

Before you listen to that voice in your head that has just piped up and said something like, "What? Design? I can't design!" remind yourself that almost every waking moment of every day you are designing—from choosing the clothes you wear to arranging the food on your plate; from deciding what music to play to organizing the furniture in your house. Designing is simply choosing elements and arranging them within a given perimeter—you do it all the time.

The most important thing to remember as you are creating your own designs is to make something that pleases *you*. As Joseph Campbell instructs, "follow your bliss"—it has led you this far, right?

And if you are your own harshest critic, as many of us are, remember that you're doing this because it is fun. Let that little kid in you play and explore—you may be surprised at what you accomplish when you let go of the "shoulds" and "can'ts."

---

[1] *See Bibliography (page 130) for a few of the many books about designing and using the elements of design in the arts and crafts.*

The Elements of Design

- **Line** is a narrow or elongated mark—a defining outline. Line defines and separates space as well as establishes movement.
- **Shape** is the illusion of three-dimensional space in a two-dimensional image. It is the effective use of volume and depth to create an illusion of space. Space is the area around a shape—it involves the effective use of positive (coming forward) and negative (receding) space around a form. Perceived depth and distance are also aspects of space.
- **Texture** is the visual or tactile surface of an item—it is the contrasting areas of roughness and smoothness on a surface.
- **Pattern** is a discernable system of repeated motifs or images.
- **Color** is a phenomenon of light that can be described in terms of hue, saturation, and brightness.

cutting up. Go through and tear out pages with photos that appeal to you. Choose some pages that have complementary color schemes and others that use analogous colors. Look for value gradation and value contrasts. Look for texture, line, and shape.

Now take an index card and cut out a 1-inch square in the center. Use the index card as a viewfinder. Move it around one of the pages and isolate the different elements of design. You'll find that examples of several of the elements occur even in that limited space. By isolating areas, the viewfinder helps you stop looking at objects on the page and start to see the image more abstractly, so that you can see how the elements of design work. When you find something in your viewfinder that appeals to you, trace the square and cut it out.

Now look through your squares and choose squares to represent each of the elements of design and the different forms of color. Glue them to a piece of typing paper and label each element. It's fun to do this exercise with a group of friends—you'll find that each collage is unique and reveals a little about the person who created it.

Take this exercise one step further and assign feelings to each square—write about what it communicates to you.

As you work through these brainstorming exercises, allow yourself the freedom to play and give yourself permission to make something that you don't like. You may find that you like parts within the greater whole and they may spark ideas for future projects.

Using the Tools: Brainstorming Exercises

Many times, the challenge of designing for bead embroidery is getting started. So get out your beads and try some of these brainstorming exercises—they may help you jump-start your creative engines.

One way to start is to define the space you're going to work within. Create perimeters for yourself.

- Choose a limited palette of bead colors—work with a range of analogous colors of different values, or challenge yourself to work with complementary colors, or consider working with colors you don't like.
- Play with transitions between colors or values.

Start with a dark shade of a color and gradually move to a light shade of the same color. Or try transitioning between opaque beads and transparent beads of the same color and value. Or start with a saturated color and gradually transition to its muted complement.

💧 Find a bead you like—stitch it on fabric and bead around it. Let your intuition guide you. Simply enjoy the process, have fun, and don't worry about liking the final piece.

💧 Start with a 6 by 6 inch piece of fabric, stitch a piece of acid-free interleaving paper to the underside, and sketch an outline or a line across the paper backing. Baste the outline with a contrasting color of thread and fill the area it defines or follow the basted line like a path through the piece. Build your piece from there.

💧 Make a viewfinder in the shape of a piece you want to make. Paint a piece of acid-free paper with watercolors or a thin layer of acrylic paints. Use your viewfinder to isolate an area you like, and then follow the directions on page 59 to make a beaded pin.

Color

Hue is the color—red, yellow, or blue, or the infinite mixtures of these primary colors with each other and with black, white, and gray. A **saturated** hue contains no black, white, or gray.

Value is the lightness or darkness of a color. **Tint** is the amount of white in a color. **Tone** is the amount of gray in a color. **Shade** is the amount of black in a color.

Primary colors are red, blue, and yellow. **Secondary colors** are orange, green, and violet. Secondary colors are the result of mixing the primary colors—red and yellow make orange, blue and yellow make green, and red and blue make violet. **Tertiary colors** are the result of mixing one primary color and one secondary color—for example, red-orange, blue-violet, and yellow-green.

Warm colors are yellow through red on the color wheel. **Cool colors** are green through violet on the color wheel. **Complementary colors** are opposite each other on the color wheel—for example, yellow and purple, red and green, blue and orange. **Analogous colors** are right next to each other on the color wheel—for example, red-violet, red, and red-orange.

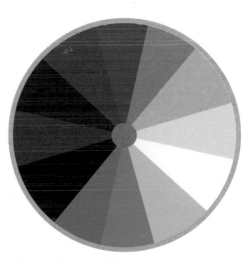

Button Soup

The possibilities of bead embroidery always remind me of the folk tale about the wealthy miser whose poor relative came to visit and offered to make lunch. The miser claimed that he didn't have the necessary ingredients even for soup—but the poor relation said that if he had a pot of water and a button, she could make her famous button soup for lunch. As she stirred the boiling button soup, she mused that with a pinch of salt the soup would be down right tasty. Intrigued, the miser managed to find a pinch of salt. After a while, she mentioned that a couple of carrots would make it even better, so the miser ran out to his garden and dug up some carrots. The story goes on and on until the poor relation has made a hearty meal—starting with a simple button.

Bead Soup

Bead soup is slightly different from button soup. Bead soup usually starts when you're working on a cloth and have poured out several small piles of beads of various colors, sizes, and shapes that you like. As you work, those beads may start to get mixed up, and at some point—maybe after you transport the cloth to another location—the beads may get completely mixed together. Some people feel compelled to stop at this point and separate the beads; others simply pour the bead soup into a small container and tuck it away in a drawer, to be excavated only when all other resources for a particular kind of bead have been exhausted. Still others forge ahead, allowing their bead soup to grow as they complete the project and move on to others.

If you're beading with a group of friends and want to add a little serendipity to your project, consider asking everyone to bring some beads to share. You'll find yourself beading with a fresh palette of beads that you may not have chosen for yourself. You'll be surprised how simply starting with unexpected beads can get your creative juices flowing.

- Draw with colored pencils, crayons, or markers, or paint directly onto acid-free paper, stitch it to your cloth, and bead it.
- Scan something you've drawn into a computer and modify it in a paint program, print it, stitch the image to your cloth, and bead it.
- Shoot a digital image (it's best to use your own images—if you use someone else's, make sure to get their permission) and print it on acid-free paper, stitch it to your cloth, and bead it.
- Paint directly onto fabric with fabric paints to create a design to bead.

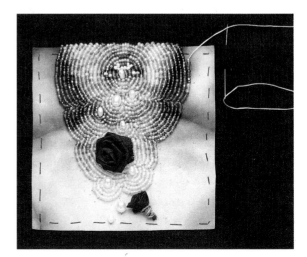

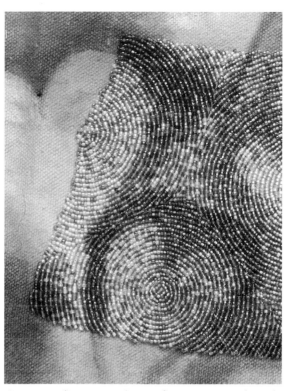

Amy painted a pre-wetted piece of cotton canvas with acrylic paints, let it dry, and then beaded the hearts using back stitch.

ROBIN'S THOUGHTS ABOUT DESIGN

Designing a project is a personal process that has many possibilities—all the way from simply winging it to drawing a detailed pattern, and everything in between.

For example, you might just begin sewing beads that you like onto your fabric, and see where it goes with no pre-planning at all. Or, you might pick a few key elements, place and sew them on, but let the rest of your beading happen spontaneously. Or, you could carefully choose the colors you want to use, and let the placement happen improvisationally. Or, you might draw a basic design and plan the colors, but let the details fall into place as you work. Or, finally, you could draw a detailed design, color it with the exact colors you desire (or use an available graphic, photo, or picture), and carefully bead the design exactly as you see it.

How much designing you do before beginning to bead depends entirely on your own preferences. All of these possibilities work well.

First of All, Please Yourself, the Artist

It's most important that you learn to recognize, understand, and please your own aesthetic taste. Sometimes we try to please someone else—our instructors, our spouses, or our concept of current fashion. However, if you don't at the same time

If you enjoy designing and planning your bead embroidery projects, these are the basic principles that I believe are important.

- Pleasing yourself
- Making sure your project is appropriate for its intended use
- Providing interest or variety, while at the same time providing unity
- Sharing a message from your heart

please yourself, you'll never like your project, never be satisfied with it, and possibly never even finish it.

It can be difficult to learn to trust your own instincts about what looks good. Even people with college degrees in art sometimes struggle when faced with design problems that don't fit the "rules" or when they sense that the rules don't "feel right" for a particular project.

However, remember that from the moment of your birth, you are surrounded by great designs. Consider nature's perfect balance of color, texture, and line in every flower, every leaf, every insect, every living thing around you—things you see every day of your life. Your subconscious takes it all in. Consider all the "art" you see in your life, even things like wallpaper, furniture, magazine ads, and online graphics, all of which were created by people with training and experience in design. Your subconscious takes it all in—every detail.

Inside each of us, there's a huge reservoir of knowledge about successful design, based on both conscious and subconscious observations. We have only to trust it to guide our intuition. Trusting your intuition is the key to pleasing yourself with your designs.

Your Design Should Be Appropriate for its Purpose

Consider who will use your project and how it will work technically. For example, suppose you are designing a little purse for your mother. Will it be large enough to hold the things she likes to carry? Does she have enough dexterity to fasten the clasp? Will it be appropriate for the type of clothes she wears?

This is the practical side of design, but one that may be overlooked easily. When the technical decisions are made about a piece early in the design stages, other aspects of design fall into place more easily, and the piece will have an integrated look.

It Must Possess Interest or Variety

Interest and variety may be achieved by providing contrasts in certain variables, such as texture, color, size of beads, value (lightness/darkness), and shape. Asymmetry is another variable that contributes to the interest and variety of your work.

Beads are made from many different materials—glass, stone, wood, plant fibers, metal, clay, plastic, and more. They come in every imaginable size, shape, color, and texture. Thus they naturally lend themselves to interest and variety.

For example, imagine a simple design like a checkerboard, with each square embroidered with size 11° seed beads. If every square had the same beads, sewn in the same direction, the results would be a bit boring. But by changing the colors and bead finishes, the resulting design would become more interesting. One square might be bright, shiny, silver-lined green beads. The next might be matte blue beads. The next might be metallic copper beads. The result could become

Experiment with Variety and Interest

Take a simple pattern, such as a 9-square grid similar to the illustrations shown here. Make several copies of the shape. Cut out small pieces of colored paper to fit the squares in the grid. Then play with arranging the colors. Keep your samples in a journal or notebook and record your impressions.

Different arrangements of the squares will change your perception of the design. In my example, you see a completely random arrangement (Figure 1), then one where I arranged the colors diagonally in a way that pleased me, with red/yellow in the top left corner, and blue/green in the lower right corner (Figure 2). Next I arranged the same colors diagonally according to their value, with the lightest in the top left corner and the darkest in the lower right (Figure 3). If these same colors were changed to a grayscale, the results would look like Figure 4.

Finally, using Figure 2 as a base, I played with patterns that can be made by sewing beads in straight lines in various directions (Figures 5 and 6). Notice the difference between these two possibilities. In Figure 5, the diagonal stitch lines on the violet and blue squares tend to isolate the three warmer colors in the top left and the three cooler colors in the lower right, so that the eye notices these corners. Because of the alternating vertical/horizontal stitching pattern in Figure 6, the same color arrangement looks much different, with the eye tending to perceive a cross.

Continue to play with your squares. Try curved stitch lines. Try different colors, perhaps analogous colors, which are next to each other on the color wheel. Try working with pastel colors only (tints), or with darker, grayed tones (shades). Try designing with some of your favorite colors and with colors you never use. What pleases you about each one? What gives the design unity? What gives it interest? For each of your samples, draw a little scale with unity on one end, variety on the other (Figure 7). Where is the balance point? Which way does the scale tip?

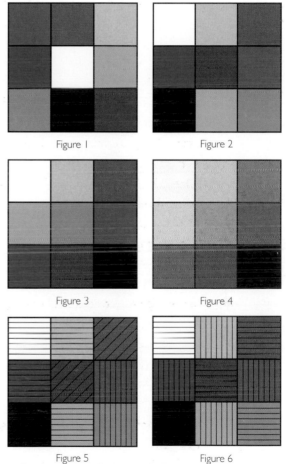

Figure 1 · Figure 2

Figure 3 · Figure 4

Figure 5 · Figure 6

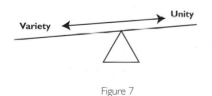

Figure 7

very interesting and pleasing, just by varying the color and finish of the beads in each square.

To achieve even more variety in the above example, the size of the beads could also become a variable. Or rather than a uniform checkerboard, the squares could be different sizes (asymmetry). Or the beads might be sewn in different directions.

It Must Possess Unity

The unity of a project makes the eyes travel around it and not want to leave it; it ties all the contrasting elements together. Sometimes unity is provided by a theme, a concept or "story" that is told by several elements in the piece. Or any of the same variables used to give interest and variety, when kept constant, will give a sense of unity to your work.

For example, consider the hypothetical checkerboard design described on page 89. If the beads in all the squares are different colors, different finishes, and sewn in different directions, the resulting design could look too busy. To give it more unity, you could use only beads with a matte finish. This one consistent element throughout the entire piece would make the journey of the eyes around the squares more sensible (or perhaps restful) to the brain.

As you can see, unity is at the other end of the scale from interest and variety. Too much variety or contrast, or too many variables, will make your project look spotty or busy; too few variables will make it look "blah." But both are important elements of design. As you look at a potential design, ask yourself, "What gives this design interest and variety? And what gives it unity?" The more you are aware of the delicate balance between these two elements, the more you will be able to make designs that please both yourself and others.

Design from Your Heart!

Most of what I've said about designing so far is "head stuff." Except for the part about pleasing yourself, it's intellectual. But another way of approaching design is from your heart. The two keys to designing from your heart are to be aware of what's important to your heart and to trust your intuition about how to tell the story.

On pages 92 and 93 you can see eighteen squares, each beaded by a different artist. Each was made shortly after the September 11, 2001, terrorist attacks on the U.S. More than 500 squares made by beaders all over the country (and from other countries as well) are now assembled into large wall hangings or "quilts" displayed in the three states that were struck by the attackers. Although most of the squares were made by individuals with little or no formal art or design training, all of them are appealing. Why is that?

Each of the 9/11 squares is designed from the heart. Every one of them tells a poignant story, a hope, or a dream. The artists are "talking" to you, telling you something about themselves, sharing

their emotions, touching yours. When you look at these squares, you feel their truth and their authenticity, which is·what makes them so wonderful.

You don't need a traumatic event of international proportions (like 9/11) to inspire work from your heart. Everybody has things in their life that are extremely important, that touch their soul at its very core—a specific relationship or person, a memorable event, a significant activity, or a special pet. In our hearts, we'd like others to know about these important things and to hear what our hearts have to say about them. Intuitively, we know how to communicate our heart messages. Our hearts know what colors, shapes, images, textures, and lines are needed to tell the stories.

Good Design Comes with Practice

Although we'd all like to create a Rembrandt or Van Gogh on our first try, it's wise to imagine how many sketches, drawings, and paintings each of those artists made before he became known. Giving yourself the freedom to practice, studying the principles of design, and analyzing your own and other's work will help develop your intellectual awareness. At the same time, you can do things like journaling, writing poetry, and meditating to develop your awareness of your heart's messages. Both will contribute to your success.

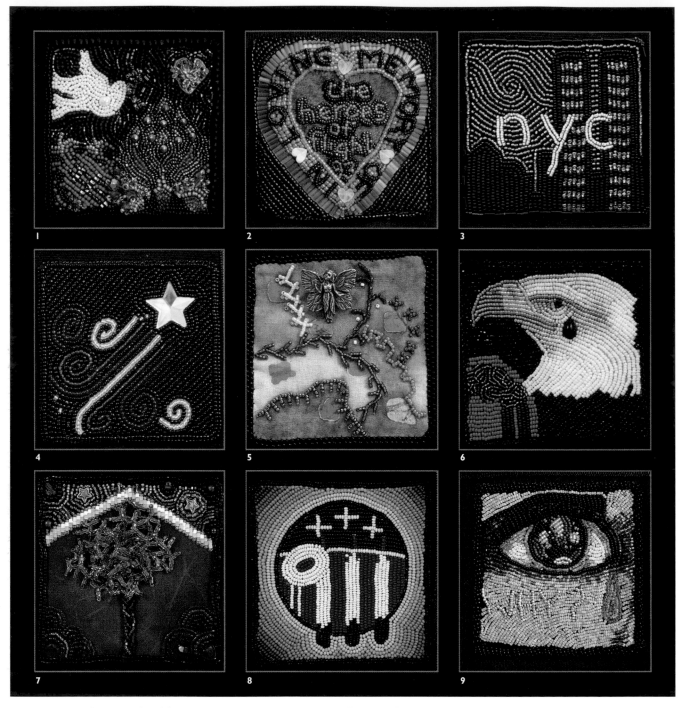

Bead-embroidered squares selected from the 9/11 Bead Quilts. 1. Jonna Faulkner, California. 2. Andrea Adams, Washington. 3. Julia S. Pretl, Maryland. 4. Tamaya Dooley, Michigan. 5. Valerie Felps, Texas. 6. Teri Packel, Alaska. 7. Cheri Zeller, Colorado. 8. Jerry Ingram, New Mexico. 9. Lisabeth Tafoya, New Mexico. Photos by Stephanie Rice.

10   11   12

13   14   15

16   17   18

Bead-embroidered squares selected from the 9/11 Bead Quilts. 10. Rosemary Greenslade, Colorado. 11. Charlene Jump, Alaska. 12. Laura Kelly, Colorado. 13. Mary Waddell, Colorado. 14. Molly Watt-Stokes, California. 15. Mary Tafoya, New Mexico. 16. Annie Laurie Burke, California. 17. Lynne Sward, Virginia. 18. Dulcey Heller, Minnesota. Photos by Stephanie Rice.

GALLERY OF BEAD EMBROIDERY

THE FOLLOWING PAGES INCLUDE examples of Amy's and Robin's bead embroidery, the work of twenty-six invited artists, and ten pieces from *Beadwork III: The Beaded Cloth* (a juried exhibit presented by *Beadwork* magazine). While all of these pieces are inspiring, they are just the tip of the iceberg. The possibilities are limitless and we look forward to seeing what you create with bead embroidery.

Amy C. Clarke, author
Loveland, Colorado

Apple with Stairs
4½ by 5 inches, back stitch using size 15° seed beads on canvas

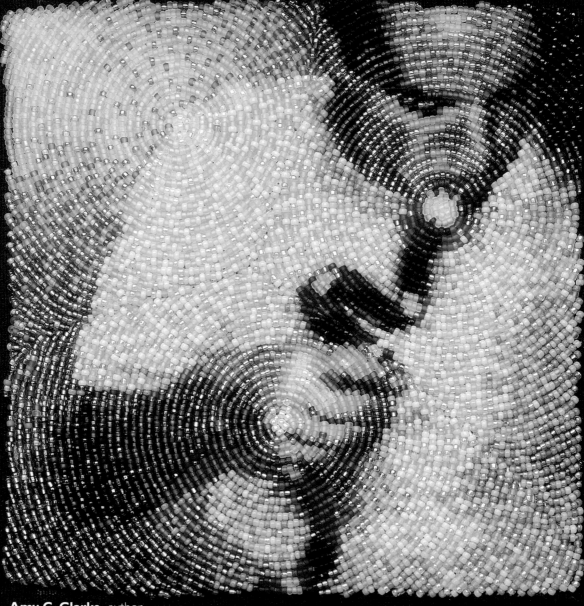

Amy C. Clarke, author
Loveland, Colorado

Kissed a Snake
4½ by 4½ inches, back stitch using size 15° seed beads on canvas
From the collection of Ana Ferrara

Robin Atkins, author
Friday Harbor, Washington

Rosie, the Uncaged Hen
Rosie, 6½ by 5½ inches, bead embroidery on fabric,
stuffed, wire armature; Rosie's Garden, 1½ by 7 inches,
bead embroidery on fabric over a wooden base

98

Robin Atkins, author

Friday Harbor, Washington

Marriage Bag
Bag 9½ by 4 by 2½ inches, bead embroidery on
fabric; wood stand 15 by 10½ inches

Chris Forsythe, *The Beaded Cloth* Exhibit
La Mesa, California

Geoffrey
19¾ by 21¼ inches, framed, back stitch
and couching on canvas

Dustin Wedekind

invited artist

Loveland, Colorado

Sleeping Beauty

8 by 10 inches, back stitch

and lazy stitch on canvas

Molly Colegrove
The Beaded Cloth Exhibit
Canandaigua, New York

A Map of the World, The Sun in Leo
11 by 14 inches, framed,
hand-painted linen beaded with back stitch

Valorie Harlow, *The Beaded Cloth* Exhibit
Chanhassen, Minnesota

Deep Within
8½ by 16½ inches, various bead embroidery
techniques and bead weaving

Jennifer Whitten, *The Beaded Cloth* Exhibit
Oberlin, Ohio

Mary
9 by 9 inches, fabric embellished with bead embroidery, crocheted rope,
and embroidery floss

Janet Dann, invited artist
Friday Harbor, Washington

Whirlwind Turtle Bag
7 by 8 inches, lazy stitch, couching, and back stitch on flannel
and canvas

Thom Atkins, invited artist
Santa Cruz, California

The Big Blue Fish Bag
9½ by 8 inches, rayon cloth embroidered with glass
beads and heishi; single stitch and lazy stitch

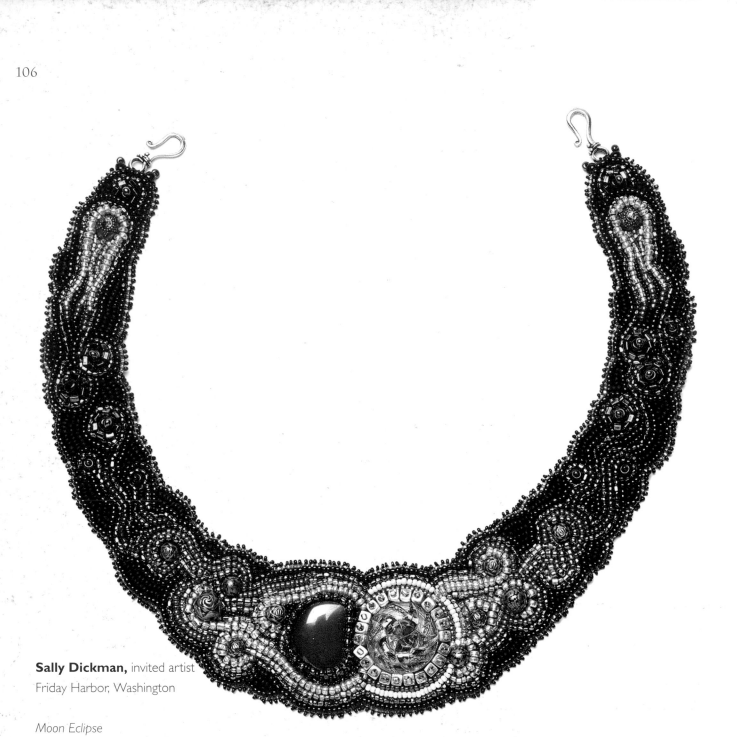

Sally Dickman, invited artist

Friday Harbor, Washington

Moon Eclipse
8 by 8½ inches, back stitch and couching on
Ultrasuede®; size 11° and 15° seed beads,
larger beads, and found objects

Rebecca Brown-Thompson
invited artist
Christchurch, New Zealand

Jurassic Garden
3 by 4 inches, bead embroidery
around a fossilized cabochon
Photo by Lloyd Park

Mary Timme
invited artist
Aurora, Colorado

The Starfish Are Coming
mask, 7½ by 5½ inches,
bead embroidery, starfish
constructed separately;
straps 8½ inches long, brick
stitch and peyote stitch

Rain Olympia Crow, invited artist
Boulder, Colorado

Squash Blossom Coat
22 by 56 inches, velvet embellished with silk
fusion, gold trim, and bead embroidery;
based on Folkwear® Turkish coat pattern

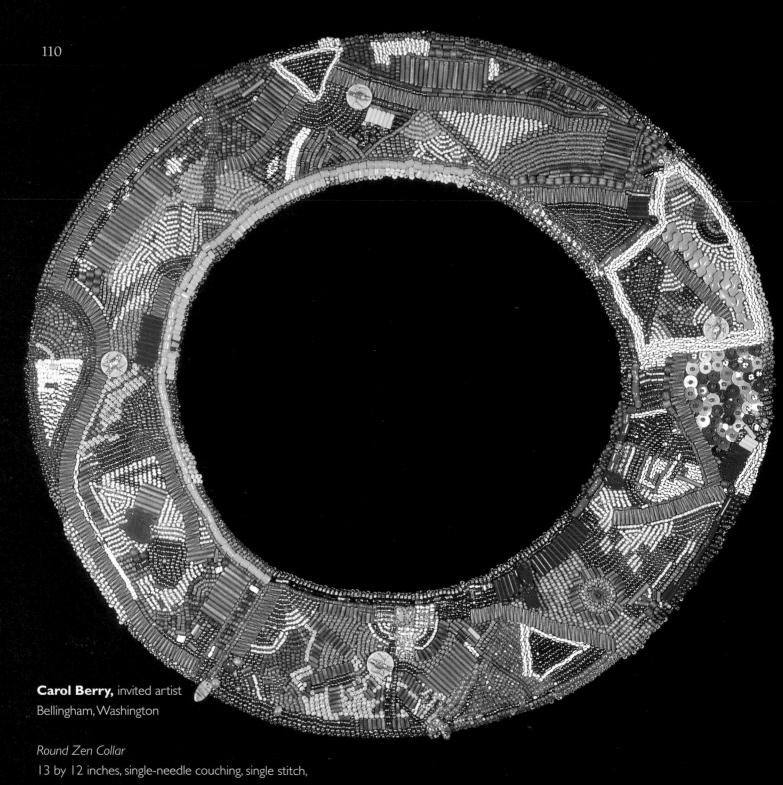

110

Carol Berry, invited artist
Bellingham, Washington

Round Zen Collar
13 by 12 inches, single-needle couching, single stitch,
and peyote stitch with a variety of beads on cloth
Photo by Paul Brower

Dorothy Loomis, invited artist
Bellingham, Washington

Grandmother's Bag
5 by 8 by 2½ inches, assorted beads and
bead embroidery techniques on a Crown
Royal® flannel bag
Photo by Paul Brower

Liz Manfredini, invited artist
Seattle, Washington

Rooster Collar
10¾ by 8½ by ½ inches,
back stitch over wire and
Ultrasuede®
Photo by Joe Manfredini

Megan Noel, invited artist
Seattle, Washington

Soul Mate Doll
box, 4 by 4 by 1½ inches, painted papier-
mâché, silk velvet and metallic fiber lining;
dolls, bead embroidery on Ultrasuede®
Photo by Jan Cook

Carol Perrenoud, *The Beaded Cloth* Exhibit
Wilsonville, Oregon

In God We Trust
3 by 5 inches, pin (framed for exhibition)
bead embroidery, coins, tokens, and paper currency

Mel Jonassen
The Beaded Cloth Exhibit
Norwich, Connecticut

Cinnamon Bay
6 by 6 inches, framed, back stitch with antique micro
seed beads

Cindi Powell, invited artist

Renton, Washington

Sea of Celebration
8½ by 15 inches, bead embroidery and wire work

Joanne Laessig,
invited artist
Cleveland, Ohio

Spirit of God
7½ by 6 inches, back stitch and
single stitch on canvas stretched
around a frame, peyote stitch
band on the sides

Terri Atwell, invited artist

Anchorage, Alaska

Working on Wings to Fly
5½ by 4 by ½ inches, stacked single stitch, bead ladders, fringe, lazy stitch, and back stitch; seed beads, vintage beads, sequins, nailheads, and metal charms
Photo by Chris Arend Photography

Valerie Thorson
invited artist
Seattle, Washington

Mandala Purse
7¼ by 5¾ inches
back stitch and couch-
ing on black raw silk,
new and vintage
pressed glass beads,
and seed beads

Mimi Holmes, invited artist

Minneapolis, Minnesota

Beloved Mine
10 by 14 by ¾ inches, Polaroid photo transfer on cloth and bead embroidery using sequins, seed beads, trim, and bugle beads

Nancy Eha, invited artist
St. Paul, Minnesota

All Things Old Are New Again
30 by 18 inches, hand pieced and stitched, bead
embroidery replicating Victorian crazy quilting
stitches and motifs; fancy fabrics, vintage lace,
vintage buttons, amber, and glass beads

Anna Fehér, invited artist
Budapest, Hungary

Small Coin Purse
3 by 5 inches, backstitch and edgings using seed
beads, bugle beads, pawa-shell pieces, and a mother
of pearl button
Photo by Robin Atkins

Gail Shen, *The Beaded Cloth* Exhibit
Columbia, Missouri

The Moon. The Sun. The Land. The Sea.
24 by 19 inches, manipulated cloth with bead embroidery

Janeene Herchold, *The Beaded Cloth* Exhibit
San Diego, California

Returning Home
16 by 18 inches, quilted cotton fabrics, bead embroidery, and thread stitching

Deb Menz, invited artist
Middleton, Wisconsin

Kingdom under the Sea
14 by 14 by 6 inches, woven tapestry, handspun and dyed silk yarn,
right-angle weave and bead woven panels, bead embroidery
Photos by Jim Wildman

Deborah Morris, *The Beaded Cloth* Exhibit Portland, Oregon

Checkered Past
22½ by 32 inches, canvas embellished with ink, dye, sequins, and bead embroidery

Jo Wood, invited artist
Hovland, Minnesota

Raven Call
22 by 11½ inches, back stitch, layering, and modified
fringe on wool fabric; suede buckskin mat; framed in
birch bark with spruce root lacing
Photo by Peter Lee

Connie Lehman, invited artist

Elizabeth, Colorado

leaf—love, lily

4½ by 6¼ by ¼ inches, bead embroidery and igolochkoy

(a Russian needlepunch technique) on silk

Photo by Roger Whitacre

Fran Meneley, *The Beaded Cloth* Exhibit
Niwot, Colorado

The Story I'm Leaving Behind, the Story I'm Becoming
12¼ by 11 inches, linen embroidered with beads, sequins, and ribbon

BIBLIOGRAPHY

Atkins, Robin. *One Bead at a Time: Exploring creativity with bead embroidery.* Friday Harbor, Washington: Tiger Press, 2000.

———. *How I Made "Rosie, The Uncaged Hen."* Friday Harbor, Washington: Tiger Press, 2001.

———. *Finishing Techniques for Bead Embroidery Projects.* Friday Harbor, Washington: Tiger Press, 2001.

Banbury, Gisela, and Angela Dewar. *Making Embroidered Bags and Purses.* London: Blandford, 1991.

Borgeson, Bet. *Color Drawing Workshop.* New York: Watson-Guptill Publications, 1984.

Box, Richard. *Color and Design for Embroidery: A practical handbook for the daring embroiderer and adventurous textile artist.* Washington, D.C.: Brassey's, Inc., 2000.

———. *Drawing and Design for Embroidery: A course for the fearful.* London: B.T. Batsford, Ltd., 1992.

Dean, David. *Beading in the Native American Tradition.* Loveland, Colorado: Interweave Press, Inc., 2002.

Dubin, Lois Sherr. *The History of Beads, from 30,000 B.C. to the Present.* New York: Harry N. Abrams, Inc., 1987.

———. *North American Indian Jewelry and Adornment: From prehistory to the present.* New York: Harry N. Abrams, Inc., 1999.

Duncan, Kate C., and Eunice Carney. *A Special Gift: The Kutchin Beadwork Tradition.* Fairbanks, Alaska: The University of Alaska Press, 1997.

Duncan, Kate C. *Northern Athapaskan Art: A Beadwork Tradition.* Seattle, Washington: The University of Washington Press, 1989.

Durant, Judith, and Jean Campbell. *The Beader's Companion.* Loveland, Colorado: Interweave Press, Inc., 1998.

Edwards, Betty. *The New Drawing on the Right Side of the Brain.* New York: Jeremy P. Tarcher/Putnam, 1999.

Edwards, Joan. *Bead Embroidery.* Berkeley, California: 1992.

Fisher, Angela. *Africa Adorned.* New York: Harry N. Abrams, Inc., 1984.

Itten, Johannes. *The Color Star.* New York: John Wiley & Sons, Inc., 1985.

Jerstorp, Karin and Eva Köhlmark. *The Textile Design Book: Understanding and creating patterns using texture, shape, and color.* Asheville, North Carolina: Lark Books, 1988.

La Pierre, Sharon. *You Can Design: An Adventure in Creating.* Arvada, Colorado: Genre Communications, Ltd., 1983.

Moss, Kathlyn, and Alice Scherer. *The New Beadwork.* New York: Harry N. Abrams, Inc., 1994.

Paine, Sheila. *Embroidered Textiles: Traditional patterns from five continents.* New York: Rizzoli International Publications, Inc., 1990.

RESOURCES

Other books by Robin Atkins are available through **Tiger Press,** 837 Miller Rd., Friday Harbor, WA 98250; tigerpress@interisland.net, or through her website, www.interisland.net/robinatkins.

Other books by Interweave Press are available through your local beading supply shop or **Interweave Press,** 201 E. Fourth St., Loveland, CO 80537; (800) 272-2193; www.interweave.com.

A Beaucoup Congé. 355 E. Fort Lowell, Tucson, AZ 85705. (520) 696-0032; sales@beadholiday.com; www.beadholiday.com.

Caravan Beads, Inc. 449 Forest Ave., Portland, ME 04101. (800) 230-8941; info@caravanbeads.com; www.caravanbeads.com.

Dharma Trading Co. PO Box 150916, San Rafael, CA 94915; (800) 542-5227; catalog@dharmatrading.com; www.dharmatrading.com.

Fire Mountain Gems and Beads. One Fire Mountain WY, Grants Pass, OR 97526-2373. (800) 423-2319; questions@firemtn.com; www.firemountaingems.com.

Rio Grande. 7500 Bluewater Rd. NW, Albuquerque, NM 87121; (800) 545-6566; www.riogrande.com.

Shipwreck Beads. 2500 Mottman Rd. SW, Olympia, WA 98512. (800) 950-4232; www.shipwreck-beads.com.

INDEX

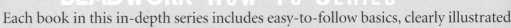

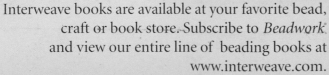